Horses of the German Army in World War II

Horses of the German Army in World War II

Paul Louis Johnson

Schiffer Military History
Atglen, PA

Acknowledgments

First of all, I thank my sister, Sharon Johnson. Thanks also go to Bonnie Blagoue and John Ryan for their help. I also thank Heinrich Jansen, who served in the German Army in WWII. In the 30th pioneer battalion on the eastern front, he reinforced bridges so heavy tanks could cross. His battalion was half-motorized and half horse-drawn. Although his main job was to serve as telephone signalman, his duties also extended to the care and horseshoeing of the unit's horses and driving a wagon. Henry answered my numerous questions on horses and horse equipment, and his memory and fondness of horses has not diminished over the years. Last but not least, I thank my uncle James E. McClelland for getting me interested in history many years ago.

Book Design by Ian Robertson.

Library of Congress Control Number: 2006920018

Printed in China.
ISBN: 0-7643-2421-7

We are interested in hearing from authors with book ideas on related topics.

Published by Schiffer Publishing Ltd.
4880 Lower Valley Road
Atglen, PA 19310
Phone: (610) 593-1777
FAX: (610) 593-2002
E-mail: Info@schifferbooks.com.
Visit our web site at: www.schifferbooks.com
Please write for a free catalog.
This book may be purchased from the publisher.
Please include $3.95 postage.
Try your bookstore first.

In Europe, Schiffer books are distributed by:
Bushwood Books
6 Marksbury Avenue
Kew Gardens
Surrey TW9 4JF, England
Phone: 44 (0) 20 8392-8585
FAX: 44 (0) 20 8392-9876
E-mail: Info@bushwoodbooks.co.uk.
Visit our website at: www.bushwoodbooks.co.uk
Free postage in the UK. Europe: air mail at cost.
Try your bookstore first.

Contents

Introduction

A lot has been written on the equipment of the German Army of WWII. Volumes have been documented on tanks, trucks, motorcycles, weapons, and personal equipment. But little has been written on the horses of the German Army that made up the greater majority of its transportation. The horse supplied about 80% of the German Army's motive power, and pulled everything an army needed in the field by wagon, or on its back. As you will see in this book, when motor vehicles failed in the mud and snow of Russia, the horse was called upon for the task. Many died in the effort.

More horses were used in WWII than in any other war in history. The German Army used about three million horses and mules from 1939-1945. More than 1.7 million died in the war. The few survivors were never to return to their homeland, but were taken by the victors.

Europe was stripped of horses for replacements, and it was never enough. Operation Sea Lion, the cross channel invasion of England initially scheduled for August 15, 1940, called for 60,000 horses. In the initial invasion of Russia—Operation Barbarossa, June 22, 1941—the Germans amassed more than 3,000,000 men, 3,000 tanks, 2,000 airplanes, and 750,000 horses.

That's a lot of horses. Just feeding that many horses seems insurmountable when one considers that a horse needs around 20 pounds of hay per day (of course, this is subject to its size and how hard it is working). But that figure demonstrates the logistical problems. Not only is the weight of hay an issue, but so is the volume. I have an average sized horse, which eats approximately 100 bales of hay during the winter months. This amount of hay takes up a space 12 ft. x 10 ft. x 8 ft. This gives you some idea of the volume. A horse eating in good pasture grass needs around eight hours of grazing to maintain its condition. This would be impossible during an advance, especially in winter.

To supplement their transportation needs, the Russian *panje* horses and carts were pressed into service. (The term *panje* horse is used throughout the book, and refers to a small Polish/Russia farm horse.) The indigenous panje was tough, insensitive to cold or heat, very tame, and needed little care. Their only drawback was they were small, and could not pull artillery or the heavy army wagons. Harnessed to their small lightweight farm carts, they could haul men and supplies through mud and snow when nothing else could get through. They proved to be indispensable. The number of horses that died during the invasion of Russia did not include the unofficial panje horse, which was not on the official rosters.

The first seven chapters of this book consist of the text from the U.S. Army Military History Institute publication MS#P-090. This little known work is the most comprehensive study I know on the subject. The topic leader and the contributors are most impressive in their knowledge and experience, and I think they say it all.

At the end of the Second World War, the Allied governments assembled groups of German POW officers to study tactics, strategy, and operational details of the war. Such studies were conducted regarding air operations, armored unit employment, and many other topics. This was done to assure historical accounting of the conflict, to determine particular problems the Germans had encountered, and to preserve the benefit of the German experience for future allied operations.

In particular, as tension between the USSR and the Western Allies grew, the German officers' study groups were asked to investigate considerations for a possible conflict with the Soviet Union in Eastern Europe. The study reproduced in part here was a product of one of these study groups, empanelled to research the use of horses both during the war, and with a view toward their possible employment during some hypothetical future conflict.

The participants were among the most knowledgeable the German Army could provide, and their conclusions constitute a critique of what will probably be the last mass use of horses in warfare.

Bear in mind as well, that if one really means to understand the performance and tactics of the *Wehrmacht* in WWII, one must understand the horse and its logistical requirements.

In the subsequent chapters, I show some of the equipment used by horse-mounted troops, as well as actual photographs of the era. I hope this book will shed some light on a seldom-addressed topic, and be of interest to the student, collector, and lover of our faithful friend—the horse.

1

Horses in the German Army 1941-1945

by *Generalmajor* Burkhart Mueller-Hillebrand

Foreword

by *Generaloberst* Franz Halder

In preparing this study, the topic leader has drawn upon the experiences of an imposing number of experts. Its large size alone indicates the many considerations necessary to cover the subject. The numerous contributions have been well organized and convincingly evaluated to produce a valuable work.

Any nation faced with the possibility of waging ground warfare in Eastern Europe must consider the material contained here in the light of its own industrial and manpower potential, for it will readily be seen that much of Germany's experience in Russia was shaped by her lack of resources and inability to commit sufficient motorized forces. Experience has made it clear that only motorized armies are able to bring wars to a quick conclusion. Modern armies must be organized for rapid movement, for which technology must provide motors adapted to every possible theater of war.

The question is asked whether the forests and swamps of the East might not be bypassed, thereby avoiding operations in terrain not suited to motorized movement. If the *Wehrmacht* could have forced a military decision by sweeping northward from southern Russia, with its right wing roughly along the Volga, the extensive swamps and forests of the north would have been avoided, and experience concerning the value of horses might have been different. Moreover, recent progress in atomic warfare now makes it possible to deny the enemy exploitation of sparsely populated areas. If an army can mobilize the motorized combat and supporting forces necessary for offensive operations in the East, the use of horses will be limited to only a few occasions, such as during the muddy season. The indispensable preparations for such employment are described in detail on the following pages.

The use of cavalry in the East will never be worth the expense. Mountain forces also seem to be unjustified, for no military decisions will ever be made in the Arctic or in the Caucasus.

I personally favor a solution without the use of horses. Certainly, the problem must be considered in all of its command and organizational aspects. Much will depend on whether science can develop new techniques to improve mobility. If the motorized forces necessary for operations in the East are not available, perhaps a decision could be forced by other means of war, especially those provided by a modern air force.

Ultimately, the decision whether to include horses as a regular means of transport in the East must depend on the nation's war potential. Any attempt in the course of a campaign to employ large numbers of horses without advance preparations can only lead to failure.

Topic Leader and Contributors

Topic Leader:

Mueller-Hillebrand, Burkhart, *Generalmajor*, cavalryman, transferred to the panzer forces 1942, commander of a panzer regiment in the East, chief of staff of a panzer corps and a panzer army.

Contributors:

Von Christen, Hans-Henning, *Oberst im Generalstab*, cavalryman, panzer forces as of 1942, regiment of the 1st Cavalry Division, 1941, later general staff officer attached to the panzer forces.

Feldt, Kurt, *General der Kavallerie*, cavalryman, 1941, commander of the only cavalry division in the East.

Fontaine, Prof. Dr. General veterinary, formerly Army Veterinarian in the Army High Command.

Gaggermeier, Georg, Dr., *Oberstveterinaer*, assigned to the mountain troops in the Caucasus and in Finland.

Harteneck, Gustav, *General der Kavallerie*, cavalryman, chief of staff of an army, commander of an infantry division, commanding general of a cavalry corps.

Hess, Wilhelm, *Oberst im Generalstab*, infantryman, chief of supply and administration of the Twentieth Mountain Army in Norway and Finland.

Mendrzyk, Richard, *Oberst im Generalstab*, cavalryman, *generalstaff* officer of a panzer grenadier[1] division, chief of supply and administration of a panzer army.

Munsel, Oskar, *Generalmajor*, cavalryman, later panzer forces, filled various commander positions in the panzer forces.

Von Noleken, Heimar, *Freiherr*, *Oberst*, cavalryman, commander of a Cossack regiment.

Pemsel, Max, *Generalleutnant*, mountain infantryman, various general staff positions in the mountain forces, chief of staff of the Twentieth Mountain Army in Norway and Finland

Pulte, Joseph, Dr., *Oberstleutnant*, formerly specialist in the Inspectorate of Riding and Driving of the Army High Command, at present Director for Animal Husbandry in the Rhineland Bureau of Agriculture (*Landwirtschaftskammer*).

Reichelt, Paul, *Generalmajor*, infantry, various general staff positions in the East, commander of an infantry division.

Richert, Hans-Georg, *Oberst im Generalstab*, artilleryman, operations officer of an infantry division, commander of an infantry division, commander of an infantry regiment in the East.

Von Seherr-Thoss, Hilsar, *Freiherr*, *Oberstleutnant*, cavalryman staff officer for riding and driving with an army, on the staff of the Inspectorate for Riding and Driving in the Army High Command, the commander of a *Wehrkreis* riding and driving school.

Weidemann, Gerd-Axel, *Rittmeister*, cavalryman, later panzer forces, in 1941 with a regiment of the cavalry division, as of 1942 in an armored regiment, of which he later became battalion commander.

Windisch, Joseph, *Generalmajor*, engineer, chief of supply and administration of an army and an army group, chief of signal communication forces on the staff of the Chief of Army Supply and Administration.

Von Woedtke, Joachim, *Oberst*, cavalryman, liaison officer of a Romanian cavalry brigade, instructor at a cavalry school.

Zieger, Wilhelm, Dr., *Oberfeldveterinaer*, in various posts in the East, such as veterinary officer of the 1st Cavalry Division, and of an infantry division, veterinary officer of the cavalry corps, leader of a supply project to transfer 24,500 horses from the zone of interior to Army Group Center.

Organization of the German Army up to 1941

The German Army never considered completely replacing horses with motor vehicles. Under the Versailles Treaty the 100,000 man army, which provided the nucleus of the later *Wehrmacht*, was only sparingly equipped with motor vehicles upon its organization in 1920. This capsule army comprised seven infantry and three cavalry divisions, and its entire motorized force included less than 500 men, or not even five percent of the whole. Motorization theory was studied, and limited experiments with tanks and other motor vehicles were conducted with the aid of the Soviet Union. Restrictions of the Versailles Treaty, however, made any extensive motorization impossible.

After 1935, when the reconstruction of the army was begun, iron and steel remained in short supply in Germany, despite a considerable increase in production.

This increase accompanied the vigorous economic revitalization that started to develop at that time. The economic crises of the preceding years had left the railroads badly in need of new equipment, and the large scale municipal and party construction programs initiated by Hitler also reduced the share of iron and steel available for armament production. The Army, Navy, and the newly formed *Luftwaffe* engaged in a constant struggle over the allocation of vital raw material.

The greatest part of the iron and steel available to the Army was used for constructing new barracks and other installations, for expanding the armament industry, and for high priority fortifications along the western frontier. The remainder was divided among the manufacturers of weapons, ammunition, equipment, and motor vehicles.

Because of the restricted production of motor vehicles, even the limited expansion plans permitted the Army could not be fully completed. By 1939 only a small portion of the Army's motorization program had been realized.

The problem was not confined, however, to the procurement of sufficient steel. The designing of military vehicles, such as tanks, cross-country trucks, and prime movers had recently entered a stage of rapid development after a period of stagnation. Consequently, the Army had to exercise caution, for it could not afford to order tanks and other specialized vehicles in large numbers if they would soon become obsolete. Germany's dependence upon foreign sources for motor fuel also had to be considered in deciding to what extent motorization was feasible.

Since Germany's industrial centers in Upper Silesia and the Saar were dangerously close to her borders, it was necessary for reasons of defense to attain a status of complete war readiness as quickly as possible. As the wartime army was to be three to four times larger than the active peacetime army, sufficient vehicles to meet the expanded need could hardly be held ready in depots. Once hostilities had opened, there was no choice but to acquire the necessary motor vehicles from the domestic economy wherever possible. This meant requisitioning a large number of civilian owned cars and trucks, even though they were a doubtful substitute for specially designed military vehicles.

An even more important source of transportation was the horse which, while slow, was not dependent on fuel imports or internal fuel stockpiling. Quite apart from this factor, the horse was considered indispensable by the infantry, and by all other arms in close contact with the infantry in the field. The necessity to control wide areas by means of motorized forces, or to engage in far reaching operations never occurred to the Army, whose mission was only the defense of the Reich.

Such conditions determined the extent of motorization in the German Army. Expressed in figures the picture is as follows: The Army, which in 1933 comprised 10 obsolete divisions, had grown by 1939 to 55 divisions, 14 of which were fully motorized; the activation of an additional 51 infantry divisions within a period of a few days was contemplated in the mobilization plan. Most of the GHQ forces were not fully motorized, despite the increased efforts of industry.

Each infantry regiment, comprising about 3000 men, included some 640 horses, 55 motor vehicles, and 45 motorcycles; each infantry division, comprising about 17,000 men, included some 4,700 horses, 1,000 motor vehicles, and 500 motorcycles. After mobilization at the beginning of the war in 1939, the field Army, with strength of 2,740,000 men (106 divisions, of which 14 were fully motorized), possessed 514,000 horses, 183,000 motor vehicles, and 94,000 motorcycles.

With the exception of one cavalry brigade stationed in East Prussia, the cavalry was reorganized into armored divisions. At the same time, mounted reconnaissance battalions still existed within the infantry divisions.

As the war grew in scope far beyond what had been envisioned in Germany, further reinforcement of the army became necessary. Although vehicle production had increased, it was still not possible appreciably to improve the Army's motorized equipment, owing to the very large number of civilian cars and trucks requisitioned.

During the French campaign, for example, many units used ordinary civilian passenger cars to pull antitank guns on the battlefield. At that time, of the 45,000 tons of heavy truck transportation capacity available to the army group commanders and agencies of the Army High Command, only 2400 tons were provided by regular military vehicles. Later this proportion decreased even further, as heavy trucking capacity increased to 80,000 tons.

Before the German Army began its advance into the East, the conditions which it expected to encounter were studied in detail. Three factors in particular presented new problems: (1.) scarcity of paved roads and bridges; (2.) condition of the soil in various areas and at different seasons; and (3.) vast distances, which led to isolation of forces and new supply problems.

In launching the eastern offensive, the same principles used in previous operations were retained. While the infantry divisions, which composed the bulk of the army, advanced at the speed of its horse-drawn vehicles, decisive thrusts were to be made by several strong armored spearheads tactically supported from the air. These mobile elements were to split up and encircle the enemy by means of rapid, fluid movements.

The German command expected sufficient opportunities to employ motorized forces during the favorable seasons, and believed decisive operations could not be conducted during the winter months and the muddy period. Although the first supposition proved correct, it was not true that effective operations were suspended during the winter. Fighting more or less stopped during the spring thaws, but the Russians chose to continue operations during the coldest part of the year, using forces equipped for winter mobility. During the first winter campaign the enemy presented the Germans with many unexpected situations, which the latter had to meet with all their strength to avoid annihilation.

The increasing width and depth of the advance led to the conclusion that a closely connected front could not be maintained. The result was a situation in which mobile forces capable of rapid movement became even more important. At the same time, it was necessary that all combat forces in the field be effectively mobile. While motor vehicles provided the chief source of mobility, by providing horse-drawn units with lighter equipment and additional pack animals their mobility could also be improved.

The number of motorized units was increased as far as possible. By decreasing the number of tanks in each armored division their number was almost doubled, although the total desired by the high command was never realized.

The greatly extended supply routes required a considerable increase in the motorized supply services. Stringent centralization of command was designed to utilize all supply transport facilities effectively. The sturdiest types of motor vehicles were assigned to the East, although many types planned for commitment proved unsuitable.

Because motor vehicle production could not approach the demand, special attention was paid to maintenance. Production of spare parts was increased, and maintenance facilities were greatly enlarged—projects attended by great difficulties caused by the large number of vehicle types, and the unusually long overland supply routes. The excessive strain on all vehicles in Russia was far beyond expectations, and all installations had to devote more personnel and materials to maintenance, from factories in the zone of interior, to maintenance units at the front. Still, many thousands of motor vehicles were lost in the course of the campaign through lack of spare parts and service.

The bulk of the Army continued to move at the speed of its horses and foot soldiers. To increase mobility, the weight carried by the infantryman was lightened by increasing the baggage train. Several of the infantry divisions were converted into light infantry divisions: they retained their horses, and were issued special, light vehicles designed to improve mobility in swampy, forested, or uneven terrain.

In Poland, thousands of lightweight local farm carts and sturdy farm horses were requisitioned for use in Russia. These replaced motor vehicles where terrain difficulties prevented their movement.

It was expected that cavalry forces could be used to advantage in the East. The single cavalry brigade existing at the start of the war was expanded into a cavalry division in the winter of 1939-1940. No further increase was undertaken at that time, however, for the advantages were not considered to justify the cost. In addition to its valuable horses, the cavalry division included a number of motorized elements. Moreover, cavalry units required a high degree of training if they were to prove effective in engagements against modern armament. The use of cavalry was restricted to only a few situations because of its limited shock power.

As a result of efforts to adopt Army organization to conditions expected in Russia, the 136 divisions that invaded the country in 1941 were constituted as follows: 31 panzer and panzer grenadier divisions, 99 infantry divisions, four light infantry divisions, one cavalry division, and one mountain division.

Value of Horses in the Eastern Campaign

The preparations made for the summer offensive of 1941 in general covered actual needs. Operations proceeded smoothly and effectively, even though in some instances horse-drawn units had difficulty in following the advancing armored spearhead.

The muddy period in the fall produced consequences, which were not entirely expected. Rather than curtail operations, as was done later in the campaign, the high command attempted to maintain the tempo of the advance, thereby consuming the strength of men, horses, and vehicles beyond justification. At the time this action seemed warranted by the situation, but in retrospect it appears as a costly error.

With the onset of winter the German Army suffered its setback before the gates of Moscow and Leningrad. The exhausted and overburdened troops received a severe blow to their morale. In many respects the motorized forces were in a more perilous position than were those with horses, for the boundless mud, followed by bitter cold, ice, and snow presented new technical problems, some of which could not immediately be overcome.

While motors easily stalled, horses could adjust themselves to the changing conditions, and did not leave the troops completely without transportation. Even though horse casualties were high, they occurred over an extended period, and so were less crippling. Moreover, captured horses and, in emergencies, local animals could also be pressed into service. It must be remembered in considering the value of horses, however, that many of the types of motor vehicles employed in Russia were not suited to extreme conditions.

After the first winter conditions were no longer so bleak. The troops had grown accustomed to the extreme climate. Vehicle design improved, and the drivers learned more about the operation and care of their engines. Motorized forces crossed terrain in 1944 that they never would have dared in 1941.

An added handicap in the first winter was the personal intervention of Hitler, for once the enemy had seized the initiative along the entire front, he forbade the motorized forces to use their mobility to advantage. Instead, the front was stabilized over a distance of 2,000 kilometers, from Rostov to Leningrad. The overall scarcity of troops made necessary the inclusion of motorized, as well as horse-drawn elements in the front line, where they sacrificed their mobility to a stationary role.

The horse-drawn forces were better able to adjust to the task of defending a rigid front than were the motorized units. Horses proved valuable in maintaining a stationary line even in the most unsuitable terrain, and many armored and motorized divisions turned to horses as better means of transportation under the unnatural situation in which they were now forced to fight.

Many officers and men of the armored divisions had, a short time before, been part of the cavalry of horse-drawn forces. Such men could quickly make good use of horses captured in combat, or requisitioned from the rear or from the adjacent units. Often the Russian farm horse proved useful, although only in conjunction with care and a suitable vehicle. Only the local harnesses, wagons, carts, and sleds could be used with Russian horses, and most of such equipment was in very poor condition.

The opinion that warfare in Russia could not be conducted without horses gained wide acceptance during the winter of 1941-1942. The increasing shortages of motor vehicles and fuel in the course of the campaign helped to sustain this view. Again and again units that had formerly relied on motor transport resorted to the use of horses, as the conduct of the war became increasingly influenced by Germany's lack of resources.

In spite of many cases in which horses appeared superior to motor transport on the Eastern Front, the writer is unable to share the opinion that horses are indispensable to the conduct of operations in Russia. Owing to high mobility and hard striking power, motorized forces are able to determine in large measure the terrain in which decisive engagements will be sought. Of course, much depends on how nearly industry, in producing specialized military vehicles, is able to meet the stringent demands of conditions in the East. A strong air force and ample sources of fuel are further requirements for successful motorized operations.

Supply lines must be efficient and well secured, for motorized armies are more dependent on supplies than are horse-drawn armies. The threat to supply routes, whether from partisans or atom bombs, must be met by utilizing the widest practical network of rail lines and highway, as well as by taking the fullest advantage of air transport.

While the writer maintains that horses are not absolutely necessary for operations in the East, it is not denied that horse-drawn forces are more suitable than motorized for engagements in terrain such as that found in the forest and swamp regions of central and northern Russia, and the forest and lake country of Finland. The decisive actions of a war, however, are not conducted in such terrain.

In accepting the view that horses are unnecessary to warfare in Russia, however, it is essential to understand the requirements of a completely motorized army when subjected to Eastern conditions. The expanses of Eastern Europe swallowed whole armies, and primitive roads and facilities greatly increased the strain on all equipment. The population easily adapted itself to guerrilla warfare, which required the employment of strong security forces behind the front to maintain order, and to protect the long supply lines, upon which success at the front depended.

During WWII Germany and her allies committed in Russia alone about 230 divisions, of which 35 were armored or motorized. These proved insufficient, even though the campaign never extended beyond the western portion of the country, the base of German operations lay along the Vistula, and Russia was badly weakened by the early German victories in 1941.

What will be the result if a motorized army again undertakes a campaign in the expanses of the East, if operations finally bog down, and if the initiative passes to the enemy, who by utilizing horses has made use of areas in which motorized transport is impossible? Certainly both sides would then require the use of horses. Even though many reasons favor discontinuing the use of horses, such a decision is taken only at a risk that the responsible authority would do well to consider.

It must be made clear that a fully motorized army that does not provide for the use of horses is not in a position to organize horse-drawn combat forces on short notice, if it is suddenly faced with a situation requiring them.

2

Suitability of Different Breeds

by *Generalmajor* Burkhart Mueller-Hillebrand

I. Characteristics of Different Breeds

As mounts and as light and heavy draft animals, the German Army required horses of varied size and temperament; horse breeding in Germany had produced many special-purpose types, so that a suitable breed could always be supplied. Before the warhorses were also imported from other countries, particularly Hungary and Eire. After the collapse of the West in 1940, French, Belgian, and Dutch horses were also made available to the German Army.

The cavalry mounts, which were light breeds, included horses from East Prussia, Hanover, and Lithuania (warm bloods), and a small number from Eire and Hungary. The Nordic cold bloods, native to Bavaria, were used both as mounts and as draft horses. The Russian and Polish *panye*[2] horses, also found in East Prussia, were used as draft animals. Packhorses included the Hafling, a breed that migrated into the Alps, and the various breeds of Balkan mountain horses. Mules were bred in Germany, although only on a limited scale, and were assigned to the mountain troops, as were the few available Haflings and the light Balkan breeds.

Medium breeds of horses included the German Holsteins, the East Frisian and Wurttemberg warm bloods, the Boulonnais cold bloods, and the lighter types of the French coach horse, a breed especially desirable for military purposes.

The heavy cold blood breeds were used for heavy tasks, and included the Rhenish horse, the Belgian Ardennes, and the heavy French breeds, especially the heavy coach horses.

Under peacetime conditions, and in the early part of the war, all breeds allocated to the Army were carefully separated. Wartime conditions, however, resulted in an increasing intermixture.

In general, all breeds proved effective, so long as they received proper care, sufficient grain and forage, and were distributed according to suitability. Proper care, of course, depended upon the men who handled the horses, their training, discipline, experience, and character. It was found that Central and Northern Europeans were more qualified to handle horses than were, for example, Spaniards or Italians. The Russians were not well suited to handle German horses. The importance of proper handling can be seen from the fact that enemy fire caused relatively few casualties among the horses, with most losses resulting from overexertion or lack of fodder. Both of these causes were aggravated in part by lack of understanding on the part of handlers, commanding officers, and administrative authorities.

Although few cavalry mounts were required, both warm and medium cold blood draft horses were needed in great numbers to transport loads at a fast pace. At times these horses were required to move for long distances at a trot, and for shorter distances at a canter. At the same time, all horses had to be able to serve as mounts.

In general, it was found that horses should not be too large; preferably they should be small, low-slung, broad, compact, and have a good rib structure. They should have strong bones and an energetic, spirited movement. Besides having absolute balance and good temperament, horses should be sinewy and hardy, capable of great endurance, and should not sweat too readily.

Although the heavy cold bloods required the most care, they were also able to pull the heaviest loads. If they were not to lose strength, they required regular daily rations of from 12 to 18 pounds of oats and dry fodder. Performance also diminished if heavy breeds were coupled with medium weight horses in the same team. Often it was impossible to carry along sufficient fodder, and to let the horses graze was impracticable, for to maintain health without eating oats a horse must spend eight hours each day on good grazing land. Therefore, under the conditions of the Russian campaign, the heavy cold blood breeds were hardly suitable.

Experience in Russia showed that the lighter the breed, the less forage and care necessary. On the other hand, the lighter and more spirited horse required more experienced and better trained attendants, and was more sensitive to rough treatment than was the less highly bred horse. The panye, while demanding less care and fodder, could also not pull such heavy loads. Mules proved particularly tough when treated with love and patience, although there were not many in the German Army. In addition to qualifying as a pack animal, the South African mule was suitable as a mount, while the Argentine mule could double as a draft animal.

II. Horse Requirements of the Cavalry and Motorized Arms

Greatest endurance under conditions of the Russian Front was shown by the light breeds, specifically the East Prussian, Hungarian,

Lithuanian, and Polish (half-breeds based on Arab stock) breeds, and Hanoverian and Russian purebreds. The ideal breed, particularly for the cavalry, would therefore be a highly bred horse, small and sturdy, with short legs and broad ribs.

It is recognized, of course, that German experience in handling horses cannot always be applied by other nations. An example can be seen in the Cossack Division which, except for German cadre, was composed of Russian volunteers from the Ukraine, the Caucasus, and southern Siberia. After its cavalry regiments were equipped with horses from the Don, Hungary, and East and West Prussia, it soon became apparent that only the Russian horses suited the Russian riders.

The Cossacks are natural horsemen, to whom the German school of riding is completely foreign. They are accustomed to riding over rough ground, and usually travel at a fast trot or a Cossack gallop, a gait that frequently caused injury to the legs of German horses. The Cossack is extremely interested in the welfare of his horse, and makes it his inseparable companion. But while he gives it plenty of forage, he does not appreciate the value of grooming. In the case of the Cossack Division, however, the Russian horses were the best of all the mounts, for they were suited to the Russian way of riding, and were the most hardy. Next in value were the Hungarian horses, which excelled in a firm, brisk gait. The East and West Prussian horses demanded more care and grooming, and were often too large.

Medium and heavy horses were used by the artillery as draft animals. Despite the frequently hilly terrain of France and Belgium, it was possible to pull 105mm howitzers, weighing 2400 kilograms, with a team of six horses. This number however, was soon proved to be inadequate in the East, where there were almost no paved roads. During the summer of 1941, when the horse-drawn artillery of the infantry divisions regularly covered 30 or 40 kilometers per day over hot, dusty roads, the guns often sank into sand or swamp almost to their axles. The effort of such work was more than could be asked, and after a few days the teams had to be increased by the addition of captured or requisitioned horses. This was also done in the case of infantry and artillery teams pulling supplies.

The extra horses, of course, were not working to full efficiency, and would have been more helpful if harnessed in a single span. When teams of four, six, or more horses are used, total pulling power does not increase in direct ratio to the number of horses, since each horse will pull less than if he were working alone.

In Russia the Army used a solid, roomy, steel combat vehicle, usually heavily loaded, and requiring a team of powerful heavy or medium horses. Teams for these vehicles were difficult to obtain in Russia, where lighter horses were favored, and often the armored personnel carriers were not able to follow the infantry into every type of terrain. Many infantry divisions retained their personnel carriers throughout the entire campaign, even if they sometimes served only as supply wagons. The suitability of the panye cart, which was the other extreme in weight and capacity, will be discussed in the following section.

III. Horse Requirements of the Supply and Rear Services

At the beginning of the Russian campaign, the combat trains of the infantry divisions were motorized, but in 1942 part of these became horse-drawn. The main reason for this change was the growing scarcity of motor vehicles, in some cases; however, it was made necessary by the existence of swamps and forests along much of the front in the central and northern sectors. It is true that cross-country vehicles could have negotiated such terrain, but the German supply columns were composed largely of ordinary civilian trucks. None of the trains were uniformly equipped; an average of about 120 tons of the division's 300-ton supply train were drawn by horses.

In general, all breeds could be used effectively to haul supplies, always provided that they were handled with understanding. Even the more sensitive heavy breeds stood up well if not subjected to exorbitant demands on their capacity.

Polish and Russian panye horses were employed as temporary expedients. As an integral part of the countryside, and a product of Eastern climate and culture, the panye horse came to the aid of the hard pressed German forces under every sort of situation, and quickly earned a reputation for reliability.

The panye horse is the common farm horse of the east, and as such is especially hardy and robust. They were capable of great endurance, sometimes covering up to 150 kilometers in a single day without sign of exhaustion. One and a half kilograms of oats daily were sufficient to insure top performance. Other grains, like corn or barley, could also be used. In summer most of the horses received nourishment only from grazing, while in winter they fed on mildewed hay, straw, or foliage and, when necessary, bark and thatch. While this diet naturally caused a drop in efficiency, the panye possessed a strong resistance to disease. Even such contagious diseases as glanders, strangles, or contagious pneumonia, which usually caused death to central and western European horses, were usually present only in mild, chronic forms.

The panye horse was a willing and tireless worker, and could be handled after only slight experience. Only the stallions sometimes exhibited bad temper, but only infrequently.

Certain disadvantages appeared, however, when the panye was used for military purposes, largely owing to its small size. Their slower gait and shorter steps were tiring for the rider. The length of their stride reduced the march tempo to about four kilometers per hour when trotting, compared with six and 15 kilometers per hour respectively for other horses. Without the military saddle, which for the panye was too large and heavy, they could also be used as mounts. Equipped with native saddles, or simply with blankets, they were sometimes used to carry messengers or footsore infantrymen.

The size of the panye also limited its use as a draft animal. On normal roads and trails their load should not exceed 150 kilograms. Only local carts and wagons could be used with the panye, since the shafts, traces, and centers of gravity of military vehicles, except for two-wheeled carts, were too high, thereby greatly reducing pulling power.

Because of its slower speed, both when walking and trotting, the panye horse could not be incorporated into regular horse-drawn columns without growing exhausted. When organized into separate columns and allowed a longer working day, it could cover a distance equal to other horses, since it was able to trot at its own pace for longer periods.

When the panye was introduced into horse-drawn columns, a much larger number of accompanying troops were required to accomplish the same end. The Army discussed this problem at some length in the summer of 1943. Owing to unfortunate experiences in the past, the field forces understandably desired long-term security against all possible interruptions in regular supply. They requested the systematic allotment of additional panye vehicles in order to double the supply of emergency rations, in order to increase the amount of ammunition that could be carried with a given unit, to bring forward weapons and ammunition, and to transport wounded to aid stations. To have satisfied these demands, an infantry company, for example, would have had to employ at least 15 additional men to escort the supply columns, and to abandon certain other work. If all units concerned had increased their supply trains with additional panye vehicles, about 70,000 additional men would have been involved. Conferences and experimental loading led to a rejection of the proposal to provide panyes for combat units and altering their tables of organization and equipment.

The organization of panye horses into supply columns was similarly uneconomical. A motorized supply column carrying 30 tons required about 40 men, and in closed formation was only about 200 meters long; a panye column carrying the same load would have required 240 vehicles and 300 men, and would have been 2000 meters long.

While the high command rejected all proposals to incorporate the panye horse as a regular part of the field forces, the fact remains that the panye was, and is, a valuable means of transportation under certain temporary conditions. Such conditions are certain to exist in varying degrees for any foreign army operating in Russia.

The temporary use of panye horses on a stabilized front, primarily for hauling supplies, is conceivable during the muddy periods in spring and fall, in swamps, forests, and deep snow, and in case of fuel shortage. At such times the panye becomes a valuable, indeed practically irreplaceable aid in the regular supplying of the units of a division. Usually there will be sufficient enlisted men available to assume the care and handling of the horses.

It has been pointed out that the panye neither requires great care, nor demands skill on the part of the rider. This, of course, increases its value, especially for units without experience in handling horses. The panye is accustomed to moving in single file formation. It is unnecessary to assign a rider to each horse, except to the extent necessary for the protection of the column. With the start of the lead horse the entire column begins to move, and it is only necessary that several riders be present in the middle and end in case a vehicle gets stuck, or other difficulties arise.

Experience has shown that the panye horse and wagon can go almost anywhere that an unburdened horse can go, including all but the most hazardous forests and swamps. However, the only vehicle or sled suitable is the local type, or a copy. The sleds built in Germany for use in the East were not suited to the deep snows of Russia, and were quickly turned into firewood. The poor condition of the vehicles and harnesses found in Russia made their frequent replacement necessary.

As the condition of the Army's motorized equipment grew steadily worse, many units independently organized their combat elements so that they no longer relied on motor transport. Infantry divisions found it entirely satisfactory for one or two companies of the reconnaissance battalion to be mounted on panye horses.

IV. Performance Records

1. Influence of Terrain

While the panye horse was suitable only for pulling light loads, the German horses were capable of heavier work. When handled by understanding and experienced drivers, the German horses were able to pull loads over the worst sort of roads. In deep snow or marshy terrain, however, the heavier breeds could never match the performance of the lighter panyes.

Although the terrain of European Russia is largely flat or gently rolling, difficulties to movement were presented by the soil, which in the northern and central sectors is sandy, and in the south is composed of loam-like black earth. Rain greatly increased the difficulties posed by such ground. During a rapid movement, such as the campaign of 1941, the horses frequently were overexerted, and often developed heart conditions, which made them unfit for further use. This was the most frequent cause of horse casualties in the first year of the campaign.

The panye horse never becomes overexerted, because it stops when it is tired, and cannot be made to move again until it has drawn sufficient breath. In this respect it resembles the mule or donkey.

The crossing of river and streambeds, which in Russia are often deeply incised, also demanded a great deal from the horses. Additional horses or teams were usually employed where the unpaved approaches to bridges or fords became bottomless mud-holes.

2. Influence of Climate

Horses that were first employed in summer, and became gradually accustomed to the growing cold managed to last through the winter without great strain. Of course, it was essential that they keep their long manes, tails, and winter coats.

Inexperienced drivers, and even units sometimes believed that good grooming was not a necessity, but was merely for appearance. This view was based on the fact that wild horses retain their health without being groomed, and are able to stand both heat and cold. Wild horses, however, are not an apt comparison, for they do not sweat as much as horses that pull heavy loads. Running about on the grassy steppes, wild horses do not become as encrusted with dirt as do draft horses, which must work under all kinds of weather and terrain conditions. The saying "Well groomed is half fed" again proved its validity, for the well cared for horse could be employed for a longer time than one that lacked grooming. Care of hoofs and fetlocks was especially important in preventing malanders and other diseases.

It did not prove necessary—and was usually impossible to quarter the horses indoors. Where no other shelter was available, windbreaks could be constructed from branches and boards. In Russia the woods were often too marshy to offer protection, and in summer myriads of insects made forests unbearable for horses unless a smoldering fire could be built. In winter snow huts or snow walls

Panje horses pulling sleds on the steppes of Russia.

Above and below: Even ponies were pressed into service.

offered almost as much protection as did the Finnish tents. Above all, care had to be taken that the horses, especially when sweating, were not unduly exposed to wind, or placed in drafty stalls. In isolated cases the genitals of stallions froze in the severe cold.

3. Susceptibility to Disease

Heart disease caused by overexertion resulted in high casualties among the horses in Russia. Highly bred horses were more susceptible because of their spirited temperament. The cold bloods, especially the heavier German breeds, suffered severely when their fodder was not adequate. The warm bloods, however, were in general more easily overexerted than the cold bloods.

With the above exceptions, the health of horses that received careful and understanding management remained good. The sun and dry air was healthful and strengthening, and diseases, such as glanders and strangles, were rare among horses in the field. Exposure to strangles, scab, and similar diseases were more likely to occur in the huge collecting points and depots. The utilization of every opportunity for grazing was of great aid in maintaining health. Scabs appeared readily in horses not properly cared for, and at times it assumed such widespread proportions as to affect the operations of the combat forces. An example will illustrate the general situation in the northern sector of the Eastern Front. In the period between 20 November 1942 and 10 March 1943 a corps with several attached infantry divisions was committed to the defense of a prominent salient, against which violent attacks were being launched. Movements on the German side were limited to reliefs. Under these circumstances the horses were not worked unusually hard. Grain and fodder were in short supply, but the timely establishment of rest camps for horses, and the collection of hay harvested by the Army improved the situation. The number of horses assigned to the corps totaled 39,000, of which 20 percent were regularly rotated to rest camps. Casualties for the above period numbered 3,523, of which 1,513 died of exhaustion, 1,149 from enemy fire, and 861 from other causes. Sixty percent of the horses suffered from scab.

V. Other Draft and Pack Animals

Animals other than horses were used in isolated cases, but they were never of any great significance.

Camels were used as both pack and draft animals. They could carry 120-150 kilograms on their backs, and general performance was that of a medium-size horse.

Oxen were employed in the Ukraine and the Balkans. Because they were much slower than horses, they could not be incorporated into horse-drawn columns.

Reindeer and dog teams were reportedly effective in the polar regions.

This picture was taken near the Kalmyk steppe. With the lack of fuel and trucks, the Germans used camels for transportation in addition to horses and mules. What was at first an oddity became commonplace. Notice the camel is nibbling the soldier's cap.

An officer mounted on a donkey with a makeshift saddle poses in front of camels.

Camels hauling supplies.

3

Employment of Horses

I. Cavalry

1. Cavalry Missions 1941-1945

a. Employment of the 1st Cavalry Division in 1941

Except for mounted reconnaissance battalions within certain infantry divisions, the only cavalry force participating in the campaign of 1941 was the 1st Cavalry Division. The division's training and personnel were excellent. Assigned to the 2d *Panzergruppe*[3] as its sole non-motorized force, the division took part in the advance through the northern Pripet Marshes. In this terrain cavalry was admirably suited. It was the division's mission to secure the deep right flank of the rapidly advancing *Panzergruppe*. The swamps provided natural tank barriers protecting the cavalry from armored attack. At the completion of offensive operations, which extended to the Bryansk sector, the 1st Cavalry Division was withdrawn before the onset of winter and converted into a panzer division. As such, it remained a highly regarded force until the end of the war.

The conversion of the 1st Cavalry division to armor did not result because of its failure as cavalry. It was a matter either of increasing the number of cavalry units, or of disbanding them altogether, for as special units they had many special requirements that were not easily fulfilled. Because any great increase in the cavalry would have created organizational and training problems, and because cavalry cannot develop strong offensive power, the Army High Command decided to disband the only existing force, rather than meet the special requirements necessary for its upkeep.

b. Employment of individual cavalry units up
to regimental strength in 1942-1944

After the disbandment of the cavalry division, fighting on the Eastern Front underwent a marked change. Heavy defensive fighting occurred during the German withdrawal from the gates of Moscow in December, as the initiative more and more went over to the Russians. At the same time, partisan warfare began to flare up in the German rear. Severe winter conditions, coupled with the growing scarcity of fuel, resulted in many vehicles having to cease operation in order that others could still be available at the focal points of the fighting. On more quiet sectors, consequently, the horse was given greater prominence. Cavalry could be used effectively on secondary fronts, and to secure sectors in which the terrain was not well suited to motor vehicles. It could also serve as a mobile tactical reserve, and as a force especially suited to conduct small-scale operations against partisans.

Out of necessity, therefore, several improvised light cavalry forces ranging up to regimental size were created, usually utilizing elements of the already mounted division reconnaissance battalions. During the 1942 summer offensive on the southern front, for which nearly all of the armored and other motorized forces of the army in the East were assembled, a cavalry regiment of the *Waffen-SS* and various smaller cavalry formations were employed on the northern and central fronts.

c. The activation of a cavalry corps and the
Cossack Corps in 1944-1945

After motorized equipment had been depleted at Stalingrad and in the retreat, and as operations in the East grew increasingly influenced by the lack of men and materiel, the Army High Command decided that conditions now warranted the reactivating of cavalry divisions. Two cavalry brigades, later expanded into divisions, were formed, and subsequently combined into a cavalry corps, which was committed on the central front in the summer of 1944, and later in Hungary. The difficulties in activating cavalry forces on short notice soon became evident. Although the task was made easier by the presence of numerous division mounted reconnaissance battalions and the aforementioned cavalry regiments, the activation of the corps was not yet completed by the end of the war.

An attempt was also made to activate a Cossack corps composed of Russian volunteers. Its cadre comprised the Russian volunteer troops that had been active on the Eastern Front since 1942. A Cossack division was first employed in the Balkans against the Tito partisans, and later expanded into a corps of three divisions.

2. Evaluation of Cavalry

The main advantage of cavalry is its ability to conduct mobile operations in areas where there are no roads. It is true that its ability to cover great distances quickly is much less than that of motorized forces. Still, thickly wooded or marshy terrain hinders the cavalry less than it does motorized forces, and at the same time provides protection against armored attack. The fact that artillery and heavy weapons, which may be decisive in pressing an advantage, cannot always accompany the cavalry is, of course, a serious drawback.

As to the mission and organization of cavalry, opinions vary widely. One former cavalry corps commander still favors the organization of such a corps, with several cavalry divisions for future combat in the East. Except where rapid movement over long distances is necessary, he holds that cavalry can be assigned the same missions allotted to motorized infantry. He reasoned, however, that an armored battalion and other motorized elements would have to be assigned to each cavalry division. The only essential difference between a cavalry division and a motorized infantry division, therefore, would be that infantrymen would be mounted on horseback. It would seem, however, that infantry could be transported more effectively on armored personnel carriers, which at the same time would not be a drag on the speed of armored elements.

Other former cavalrymen point out that, since the cavalry's strength is in its ability to move over terrain too difficult for motorized forces, it should be freed of all heavy burdens, and if possible all motorized equipment. Such a force, of course, would have relatively little striking power, and in normal terrain would be helpless against enemy armor.

Probably cavalry can exist in the East only as a special force, if at all. It should be confined to such tasks as reconnaissance and security (especially in forested and swampy regions), flank protection, and combating partisans and other enemy groups in areas difficult to penetrate. The cavalry should be organized and equipped with such missions in mind, and limited to brigade or division size.

The single German cavalry division that existed in 1941 was later slightly enlarged. It included the division headquarters and two cavalry brigades, each composed of two cavalry regiments, which in turn comprised two battalions. The division also included a motorized reconnaissance battalion, a bicycle battalion, a mounted artillery regiment of three light battalions, a motorized engineer and a motorized antitank battalion (three companies), a semi-motorized signal battalion, and the division supply train, partly motorized and partly horse-drawn.

The cavalry division's commander during the Campaign of 1941 made the following remarks in retrospect:

> The division still contained too many motorized elements, which hindered maneuverability. The engineer battalions should only have been semi-motorized. The bicycle battalion proved valuable, but it should have been provided with better, special-type bicycles. The motorized reconnaissance battalion, composed of a reconnaissance company, motorcycle company, and heavy weapons elements, was absolutely essential. The light recoilless guns of the artillery regiment were excellent, and could follow the regiment everywhere. Motorized heavy artillery should be available for emergencies. Antitank battalions should have armored guns on self-propelled mounts, rather than horse-drawn guns. It was necessary that most of the combat train and part of the supply train be horse-drawn in order that the division could separate itself entirely from its motorized elements.
>
> The cavalry divisions and the Cossack Division activated in 1944 were organized similar to the 1st Cavalry Division. At first the Cossack Division was organized into six cavalry regiments, without bicycle battalions. Because this proved unwieldy, when the division was enlarged into the Cossack Corps each division contained only three cavalry regiments.

3. Experience with cavalry

In 1941 the 1st Cavalry Division fought as part of the 24 *Panzergruppe*, which was subordinate to Army Group Center. The *Panzergruppe* advanced eastward, just north of the Pripet Marshes, a swampy region 350 kilometers long and 150 kilometers wide. It was the cavalry division's mission to cover the *Panzergruppe's* deep right flank by advancing through the northern part of the marshes. Initially there was no contact on the right, for the left wing of Army Group South was moving eastward south of the Pripet in order to avoid the swamps. Within the limits of its mission, and during the continuation of the advance as far as Bryansk, the 1st Cavalry division was occupied with such tasks as flank protection, enveloping pursuit, security of wide areas, and mopping up in large forests. The division proved effective as a connecting link between the spearheading armor and the slower infantry divisions and, as such, crossed terrain that would have been hardly passable to motorized equipment.

Although the performance of the 1st Cavalry Division was exemplary, experience proves that its missions could have been performed by a motorized division with equal chance of success.

A further example of cavalry in action may be taken from the employment of the Romanian 8th Cavalry Brigade on the Crimean Peninsula at the end of 1941. The brigade's ability to move rapidly 100 kilometers in 24 hours was effective in protecting the coastline. The cavalry officer who describes the action concludes that a motorized force could have carried out the first part of the mission, but not the second part, which required a further advance of 100 kilometers over roads suddenly turned muddy by a rapid change in weather.

The non-divisional cavalry battalions and regiments scattered along the Eastern Front proved especially effective against partisans, particularly when the fighting involved rugged terrain. The cavalry corps, on the other hand, found few suitable opportunities for commitment, for the enemy employed his superiority to more or less determine the areas in which fighting was to occur. For that reason, the cavalry corps headquarters was also assigned motorized elements and infantry divisions in addition to its cavalry forces.

Only limited experience is available concerning the vulnerability of cavalry to air attack, for the Russian Air Force never appeared in the same strength as did that of the Allies in Western Europe and Italy. Evidence is that the cavalry could quickly elude air attacks by dispersing. The Hungarian cavalry division, which was attached to the cavalry corps for a period in 1944-1945, could never learn to disperse rapidly enough, or to avoid the roads. Air attacks were naturally more effective during the winter, when deep snow prevented dispersal. Horse-drawn vehicles of a cavalry were also less easily set on fire by air attack than were motor vehicles. Partisans seldom attacked cavalry formations, for they knew them to be especially dangerous.

Late in the war the Cossack Corps was committed in the Balkans against the Tito partisans. Its primary mission was to secure the valleys of the Sava and Drava rivers against attack from the mountains. Attempts to eliminate the partisans by invading the mountains were never successful. The precipitous, chalky terrain was not favorable for deployment, and the columns of cavalry and horse-drawn vehicles were easy targets for surprise attacks by enemy forces familiar with the country. Moreover, the Cossacks, like all Russians, preferred fighting en masse rather than as individuals, in which case they were likely to panic. The fact that the bareback-riding Cossacks were expert horsemen was not enough to compensate for the unusual ruggedness of the terrain. Consequently, the cavalry moved too slowly to prove effective against the well-entrenched partisans.

The Cossack Corps thereupon determined to meet the partisans on the plains. When the efficient mounted reconnaissance forces discovered the enemy leaving the mountains on a raid, they cut off retreat by surprise maneuver and forced the partisans into open battle. This same procedure was used effectively on several occasions. The chief problem was in outwitting a clever foe, who had many sources of information among the native population.

A commander of one of the Cossack divisions believes that the same mission could have been carried out by armored forces with better results. The success of the 1941 Balkan campaign, in which the Yugoslav Army was quickly destroyed by German panzer forces, would seem to argue against necessity of cavalry. Even though armor was not able to penetrate every hiding place, its rapid action sharply limited the areas over which partisans were able to hold control. This was particularly true because there were no large forests or swamps such as exist in Russia.

4. Cavalry Equipment

The cavalry mounts should be relieved of as many burdens as possible. All opportunities for decreasing the weight of equipment carried by horse and rider should be examined. It is important that riders be selected by height and weight, a consideration not always heeded by German cavalry units.

German experience shows that in Russia only light carts and wagons should be used, even though this results in longer columns. The cavalry corps in Hungary, on the other hand, desired heavy wagons and four-horse teams, as well as a large number of motor vehicles in its supply train. Both preferences are explained by the denser network of good roads in the Balkan Peninsula.

II. Infantry

1. Combat Units

Within the German infantry division the horse was the primary means of transportation in the combat zone. Motor vehicles were generally used for transportation outside the combat zone, and for staff messengers. The divisions also included motorized antitank battalions and companies, as well as motorized engineer companies.

Infantry regiments possessed a number of motorcycles in the regimental and battalion staffs, and motor trucks in the supply train to carry ammunition, explosives, and equipment. All combat vehicles and heavy weapons, as well as the field kitchens and part of the supply train, were horse-drawn. Officers in command of these columns were mounted. A very effective mounted platoon was organized for reconnaissance and liaison.

The degree of maneuverability in open country, the divisions of rate of speed, and the functioning of the supply services within the combat zone were all dependent upon the horse. An infantry Regiment of three battalions was normally assigned 641 horses and 204 carts and wagons.

Each of the reconnaissance battalions of the infantry divisions were organized differently. Their core consisted either of two cavalry troops or two bicycle troops, or one cavalry and one bicycle troop each. Each of the battalions also included an armored reconnaissance platoon and heavy weapons elements. In mounted reconnaissance battalions the heavy weapons were horse-drawn, while in bicycle reconnaissance battalions they were motorized.

The artillery regiment consisted of three horse-drawn light battalions, each with three batteries of 105-mm field howitzers, and a heavy battalion with three batteries of 150-mm field howitzers, which were usually horse-drawn, owing to the lack of motor trucks and prime movers. As to the light battalions, not only were the gun and ammunition sections horse-drawn, but also the combat trains, field kitchens, and part of the supply trucks.

In the engineer battalion, one of the three engineer companies, the bridge column, and the light engineer equipment columns were motorized, while remaining elements were horse-drawn. The antitank battalion was completely motorized. The signal battalion was partly motorized and partly horse-drawn. The division headquarters was motorized, but included a cavalry section of six mounts.

Where motor vehicles were lacking, certain normally motorized elements, such as the antitank and engineer companies, were horse-drawn. The light infantry divisions were equipped with lighter combat vehicles and one-span carts for the transport of heavy machine guns, mortars, and ammunition, in order to more easily negotiate difficult terrain. Their stock of horses was correspondingly larger.

In general, the organization of the infantry divisions proved effective. The growing shortage of manpower, however, forced either the dissolution of one of the three infantry regiments, or else their reorganization to include two instead of three battalions. To compensate for this change, the reconnaissance battalion was usually reinforced to full battalion strength and reorganized into a headquarters battalion (*Fuesilierbatallion*), which became a reserve of the division commander. This was possible after the creation of a continuous front left little need for a reconnaissance battalion. During the muddy seasons, the bicycle elements had to turn to wagons or trucks; in some cases they were supplied with light trucks, such as the wartime Volkswagen.

Despite the weight of its guns, the light artillery was always able to complete its mission. The heavy horse-drawn artillery, on the other hand, was always a problem, because the guns were too heavy for the horse teams.

2. Supply Services

It is inconceivable that a modern army operating deep in Russia could be supplied solely by horse-drawn trains. Moreover, because of their different rates of speed, horse-drawn and motorized supply vehicles cannot normally take part in a common mission. Horses, however, were well suited to hauling supplies over short distances, such as were involved in relaying supplies between depots close to the front and the units fighting in the lines.

The shortage of suitable motor trucks, however, encouraged the use of horses even further in the rear, particularly during periods of deep mud and snow. In isolated cases, horse relay systems were even used to cover great distances. Horses were also used for short hauls by rear area supply depots when no motor vehicles were obtainable. In general, horses proved satisfactory for hauling supplies wherever they were employed to cover short distances.

As the campaign continued, and as more suitable types of motor trucks arrived at the front, the drivers learned better how to drive under Eastern conditions, and how to keep their vehicles in running order. Except where fuel was lacking, complete paralysis of a motorized supply column was rare. A truck creeping painfully forward was still far superior to a horse-drawn vehicle. Eventually the fuel shortage became chronic, however, and the horse grew in significance.

In southern Russia, there was no question whether horses or motor vehicles were better able to carry supplies, even during the winter. In central and northern Russia, Finland, and Karelia, however, terrain and weather conditions were such that the division supply trucks were sometimes forced to abandon motor trucks and turn to horses as a temporary expedient.

The combat vehicles, light artillery columns, and ammunition sections of infantry divisions were also horse-drawn for practical reasons, for they had to follow the troops into battle positions at any time. It is true that well designed cross country motor vehicles could also have served this purpose, but then they would have not been used to full capacity when accompanying the slow moving horse-drawn elements of the division. Moreover, the noise of engines near the front was always a disadvantage, for the Russians reacted quickly to such warnings at night.

Motor vehicles were assigned to the infantry divisions not when they were available, but only when they constituted an essential advantage; otherwise, they should be concentrated to form the largest possible number of fully motorized divisions. That this could be done is shown by the following example. When the war began in 1939, the infantry divisions in East Prussia were equipped with fewer motor vehicles and more horses than were the infantry divisions in the rest of the Reich, yet their maneuverability was equal, since all of the divisions necessarily moved no faster than their horse-drawn elements. Infantry divisions in East Prussia were equipped with 6800 horses and 393 trucks, infantry divisions in Germany proper with 4800 horses and 668 trucks; thus 2000 horses replaced 275 trucks in each East Prussian division. Since a motorized infantry division at the time possessed 1700 trucks, six or seven infantry divisions provided with a larger number of horses released enough motor vehicles to equip one additional fully motorized infantry division.

The necessity of using local horses and local carts and wagons during periods of unfavorable weather caused the field forces to accumulate excessively large trains. At the same time, if supply shortages became evident, the troops grew suspicious that they might not receive everything they needed, and began hoarding scarce items. The accumulation of equipment diminished the flexibility of the divisions, and had to be checked by strict supervision.

3. Equipment

Too much stress cannot be placed upon the necessity to limit the weight of equipment accompanying forces in Russia. Strict weight limitations must be established for both horse-drawn and motorized vehicles. The German horse-drawn vehicles used in Russia were basically too heavy for the unusual terrain and weather conditions that are inevitably encountered. The local vehicles best suited to the terrain were the panye carts for use with small horses, and the Russian military wagons for use with normal size horses.

It was shown at once that no advantage was gained by overloading a vehicle. Two vehicles with normal leads were preferable, even though additional personnel and longer march columns were thereby created. It was also necessary that all vehicles be allowed extra time to negotiate steep defiles.

Considerable difficulties were presented by the necessity of using sleds in winter. German models were usable only on traveled roads, and therefore practically worthless in Russia. Only the panye sleds with wide runners could be used in deep Russian snows.

The German 105-mm howitzers were designed on the principle that firepower is more important than mobility, and were consequently rather heavy for use in the East. The light artillery was sufficiently mobile, although fresh horses and additional manpower were often required.

Harnesses especially designed to fit the small panye horses had to be manufactured, since the Russian harnesses were seldom strong enough or in condition to meet military demands. The panye horse performed farm work unshod, but military service made shoes necessary. Since there were no horseshoes small enough in the German Army they had to be especially made in the zone of the interior.

4. Protection Against Air and Partisan Attacks

Horse-drawn vehicles were seldom subjected to air attacks. Where they occurred, casualties remained low because the light vehicles could easily deploy off the roads.

Where danger from partisans was present, columns were provided with additional escorts. Cavalry and other mounted units composed of Russian volunteers proved especially effective for escort purposes. It was important that the columns be well armed, especially with machine guns.

The men of the supply trains had to be reliable and fit for combat. The practice common early in the campaign of assigning misfit personnel to the supply services soon produced disastrous results and had to be abandoned.

III. Mountain Troops

1. Missions

The only area encountered during the Russian Campaign that demanded commitment of fully trained mountain troops was the Caucasus. The Balkan, Carpathian, and Crimean Mountains and Lapland were accessible to regular infantry. Apart from the Caucasus, the only mountains requiring the use of mountain troops would have been those along the southern border of Asiatic Russia.

As part of a fully motorized army, mountain division had to transport its pack animals by motor vehicle. The large amount of motorized and special equipment necessary prevented the wider use of mountain troops. It was found that only small units for special missions could be profitable transported by motor vehicle.

Especially in the mountains, fighting is apt to break out initially along or near roads. The combatant with a road behind him possesses an advantage. Not until later does the fighting usually penetrate roadless terrain, at which time the advance will be slowed. The larger the unit, the sooner will this stage be reached.

Since major combat tends to take place among roads, or in areas to which access is not difficult, infantry divisions are generally capable of conducting all necessary combat missions; mountain divisions being necessary only in the case of extreme terrain or climate conditions. The larger the mountain force, the greater are the difficulties likely to occur, for the command must control four means of transportation—foot, motor vehicle, and pack and draft animal. So many types of movement lead to a splitting of forces and weakening piecemeal commitment. Where roads are inadequate, the great number of pack animals (which every 10 days consume fodder equal to the weight of their load) become an intolerable burden.

On the basis of German experience, a reinforced mountain infantry battalion is the largest sized unit practical for operations in European Russia. Such a unit might be comprised as follows: a battalion headquarters with signal and reconnaissance platoon; four mountain infantry companies; a mountain artillery battery or heavy mortar company; a mountain antiaircraft company; a mountain transportation company; and a supply section.

The unit should be fully motorized for normal movement; the use of motor vehicles especially designed for mountain conditions should hold the number of necessary pack animals to a minimum. As GHQ reserve, the unit would be assigned by the Army High Command according to theater wide requirements. Several brigade staffs might be provided for use both as training and operations staffs, the latter in case several mountain units were combined for a larger mission.

2. Animals with Mountain Troops

Since normal size horses were not suited for use in the mountains, the mountain troops were provided with a special stock. Only small, powerful horses with calm dispositions and suited to carrying heavy loads could be used as packhorses. Breeds that were used successfully were the Hafling, a native of the Alps, the Norwegian mainland fjord horse, the Hunsul, the Bosnian, the Mur Island horse from the Balkans, and the Kabardinians from the Caucasus. In emergencies the less suited Russian or Polish panye horses were sometimes used. Crosses between stallions and female donkeys were weak and unreliable, whereas the best pack animals proved to be crosses between male donkeys and mares, especially when they originated in countries where the climate was similar to that of Russia.

Pack animals could also be used to draw carts or wagons, although that task was usually assigned to heavier horses. To maintain a reserve of pack animals, and to protect them from overexertion or pack sores, it was often practical to employ them as draft animals.

Both the pack animals and their drivers must be especially trained in order to secure maximum efficiency.

3. Equipment

If the light, four-wheeled horse-drawn vehicles broke down, the local light farm and rack wagons could nearly always be used instead. They may also be utilized when the terrain or the tactical situation requires an increase in the number of vehicles.

Of particular importance was the systematic equipping of units with specially built carts. The best model was the Austrian wooden mountain cart, which could easily be altered to suit different needs. Metal carts of the Swiss Furgon type were less practical.

The German breast harness proved excellent in all cases, for use with both wagons and carts. The collar harness was a poor substitute because it was less adjustable, and its use was dependent on the physical condition of the horse. The packsaddle was the most important single piece of equipment; the German model was satisfactory, although somewhat heavy.

In winter, carts and wagons were replaced by sleds. The local types always proved to be the most suitable. Sleds should be nonrigid, curved high in front, and should have fairly wide runners. The question whether a single pole or twin shafts are better is not easily answered. Good experience was had in both cases, or even with none at all, in which case the horses were harnessed directly to the sleds. Sleds can very quickly become overloaded. Care must also be taken that loads are tightly fastened.

An excellent device, a kind of drag copied from the Russians, was constructed for transporting material over marshy ground, or during periods of thaw. The trunks of two medium-sized saplings were cleared of all but their top-most branches to serve as shafts, between which a horse was harnessed. The central sections of the saplings were connected by cross-boards, which formed a platform for the load. The top branches provided a natural spring action, allowing the vehicle to sweep over ground obstacles. These devices proved especially useful for carrying casualties.

Large wheeled vehicles and guns were systematically equipped with sled runners, which could then be installed when necessary. This helped to save the strength of the horses, for the runners could be used as soon as conditions made wheels no longer practical. Effective, standardized sled runners were developed for many guns, including those of the mountain infantry. Runners did not interfere with the firing of the weapons.

Snowshoes for horses were used only in rare instances, so that little experience was gained. When pack animals sank into the snow up to their stomachs, there was no alternative but to shovel them out. Storm driven snowdrifts could put an end to all activity.

In winter, horses were equipped with cleats that screwed into the horseshoes. Pack animals were fitted with sharp, H-shaped cleats, which afforded good stability. When icy stretches were crossed by pack columns, the horses' cleated hoofs cut up the ground so as to improve the traction for motor vehicles following behind.

4. Organization

Because under many circumstances animals restrict the division's mobility, and because they require care by trained personnel, animals should be replaced by motor vehicles whenever possible. Small vehicles especially designed for use in mountainous terrain can bring about sharp reductions in animal quotas. In Germany, the Austro-Daimler Supply Train Vehicle, the Stoewer and Hanomag mountain motor vehicle, and the half-track motorcycle were all developed for use in difficult terrain. Except for the latter, however, there was no sufficient industrial capacity to permit mass production.

In certain cases, each of the elements of the mountain forces were both motorized and non-motorized: artillery was organized into motorized artillery and mountain artillery, and engineers into motorized engineers and mountain engineers. Where this was not the case, it was advisable to have semi-motorized arms (communications, medical companies) that could be easily divided into motorized and non-motorized, or mountain units. For supply purposes, the strictly mountain elements of several arms were sometimes combined under a uniform command. The formation of task forces was also facilitated by the ease with which the various arms of a mountain division could be split into motorized and non-motorized or mountain elements. Forces employing pack animals will find these suggestions useful:

a. Each unit should have a feed supervisor, whose chief function is to act as responsible non-commissioned officer for all horse matters. In addition to the horse attendants, several non-commissioned officers may be appointed solely as section commanders (mountain sections, valley sections, and supply train sections). One non-commissioned officer should be responsible for from nine to 15 animals.
b. Pack animals should not be utilized for more than one type of load at a time. Weapons, ammunition, water, fodder, and other items are best carried separately.
c. The German mountain troops did not use pack animals to carry rucksacks and other individual equipment, except in the case of officers. The additional animals necessary would have made the mountain troops even less flexible. Moreover, it is clear that each man must have his own equipment close at hand, for to a great extent the mountain infantryman is an individual fighter.

4

Selection and Training of Personnel

I. Selection

1. General Requirements

The rural population of Germany provided an inexhaustible reserve of personnel fitted for service in mounted or horse-drawn units. Among urban dwellers were many who knew how to handle horses because of their occupations or sport activities. There were also those who asked for service in mounted units only because of their affection for animals, but who otherwise lacked training or experience.

Consisting predominantly of horse-drawn units, the German Army in World War II required some 5000 veterinary officers, or about half the total number of German civilian veterinarians. The practical country veterinarians were more suited to military demands than were those from the city, who treated mostly house pets. There were always enough elderly men available to serve as assistants to the veterinary officers.

The fear that increasing mechanization of agriculture would result in a shortage of qualified personnel was unfounded, for even the farmer who has converted to motor power will retain an understanding of horses from the nature of his occupation, and from his familiarity with other animals. At the same time, the increasing motorization of the Armed Forces will lessen the demand for men experienced with horses.

2. Physical Requirements

While physical requirements normally vary between the different arms, the harsh conditions of the East demanded greater physical vigor on the part of all personnel. Men in the service arms who were not able and eager to perform their duty in all weather, and under the most trying billeting conditions, only undermine the striking power of the technical forces.

Cavalry personnel must be selected with special care. They must be small and light, well coordinated, and mentally alert. They should be able to swim, and should not wear glasses. City dwellers are often especially well suited to riding. The lightweight of the cavalry horse makes it necessary to fit rider to mount.

In the infantry, the personnel required for horse management were drawn from within the units. Selection of horse and rider was determined by the mission. The horse was selected for the rider, and his equipment, whether it was the battery commander's binoculars or radio.

As in the infantry, artillery horses and riders must be selected according to the individual task to be performed. Drivers must see that sturdy horses are chosen to draw the heavy guns, and the men that lead these horses must themselves be capable of great strength. The riders on the lead horses should be well trained to choose the proper route. Drivers should be older men with even temperaments, and a love and understanding of horses.

The mountain troops should be assigned special personnel as animal handlers.

Civilian farriers can be selected to serve in the veterinary service, but they must first be given personal military training, including cavalry training.

II. Training

1. Peacetime Training

Wartime experience demonstrated that training in peacetime had not yet sufficiently broken away from the time when cavalry took an active part in combat, and artillery was wheeled into position without regard for cover. Valuable time was lost in the later training of personnel in the methods of modern motorized warfare.

In the interest of weapons training, which is of primary importance, instruction in riding and driving should be limited to the following objectives:

a. Horse handlers should develop an attitude of devotion for their horses, and should be imbued with the necessity for giving them proper care, even under the most trying circumstances.
b. Regard must be had to the proper methods of saddling and harnessing, and to the care of equipment.
c. The driver must have the fullest possible control over his horse and vehicle under all conditions. He should be especially trained to surmount terrain obstacles. Show riding is important only to the extent that it helps to attain the above goals.

Horse breaking and training, when combined with a constant

effort to gain and retain the horse's confidence, is more important than has commonly been realized in peacetime.

The driver must learn that some of the worst terrain difficulties can be overcome by maintaining a steady pace and constant pulling strength. In a military operation, horses normally advance at a walk, and attain their goal by a slow and steady pace. Progress should be achieved less by a rapid gait than by adhering to a carefully planned time schedule.

Particular attention must be given to the training of pack animal drivers. Because of the more difficult terrain in which they must operate, the drivers must receive more detailed instruction in loading and unloading techniques, determining performance records, and care and use of specialized equipment. Each pack animal should be assigned a driver, whose only other task is that of defense. Attempts to save on personnel by tying animals together in a column were never successful in the combat areas, where sudden enemy fire, or such terrain obstacles as mine fields were likely to be encountered.

2. Wartime Training

a. The Field Army

Even with the best peacetime training, new experiences will be gained in war, which must be introduced into training programs as quickly as possible. While this was done, however, the German Army found that its training standards sank rapidly, especially during the Russian Campaign, owing to casualties and the need for rapid replacements, the transfer of personnel, and the activation of new and reorganization of old units. Consequently, a constant training program was necessary to ensure a continued supply of qualified drivers and cavalrists, for the army was growing increasingly dependent upon horse power for mobility.

To ensure adequately trained driver personnel in the newly activated divisions, a training detail from one of the *Wehrkreis* riding and driving schools was attached to each of the new divisions for a limited period. Each of the *Wehrkreis* schools was always to have a detail available for such assignments.

All training concerning horses must be continued in the field, and intensified during periods of position warfare and between campaigns. Experience showed that some German commanders did not realize the importance of continued training, and failed to give it the attention it deserved. Increasing motorization will further obscure the need for training with horses, even though their use might become necessary. Immediately after the beginning of WWII, the Army High Command found it necessary to establish a special organization to care for horses. This organization was enlarged at the beginning of the Russian Campaign.

b. The Replacement Training Army

The fact that each field unit of the German Army had its own replacement unit in the zone of interior made it easy to transmit front line experience to the Replacement Training Army. This was accomplished by the direct transmission of reports, by visits of the reserve unit commanders to their corresponding front line units, and by regular exchanges of training personnel between field and replacement units. The front line commanders desired high quality personnel in their replacement units, and even released some of their own men to serve as instructors in the zone of interior.

c. Indigenous Personnel

Some system must be devised for training local personnel that are enlisted as auxiliary labor. This is comparatively simple, since usually a peasant and his team are enlisted for service together. To guard against spread of contagious diseases among these horses, the owners must be encouraged and instructed in giving them proper care commensurate with military standards. Drivers must be taught to move in columns, to disperse in case of danger, and to group according to signals. Once indigenous laborers have learned their jobs, the cadre personnel can be decreased in number. It is desirable that auxiliary labor be given some degree of freedom and responsibility. Rather than create an impression of hard-handedness, it is better to risk the chance that a few individuals may shirk their work or disappear, for the Russian peasant showed himself very sensitive to unjust or disrespectful treatment. By displaying a fair and friendly attitude, much can be learned from the local inhabitants, such as how to overcome the obstacles of winter without technical aids, and where to find locally known winter trails. In general, where the proper treatment was offered, local auxiliary personnel proved equal to their tasks, and were often of great value in times of crisis.

d. Eastern Volunteers

As with indigenous labor, those Russians who volunteered for service in the German Army were sensitive to rigid discipline. It was important to create mutual confidence between German cadres and volunteer personnel by giving the latter a feeling of freedom and responsibility.

III. Instructor Training

As the war progressed and casualties mounted, more and more personnel had to be trained in the care and use of horses. On the initiative of both the High Command and the lower command echelons, new training courses were established, and information and instruction pamphlets were distributed.

Ausgabe 1938

Prior to 1935, as much as 3,000 hours of rider training was given to a cavalry trooper, whose enlistment was 12 years. After 1935, this was reduced to an average of only one hour per day.

Remount training.

Mountain troops with their pack animals.

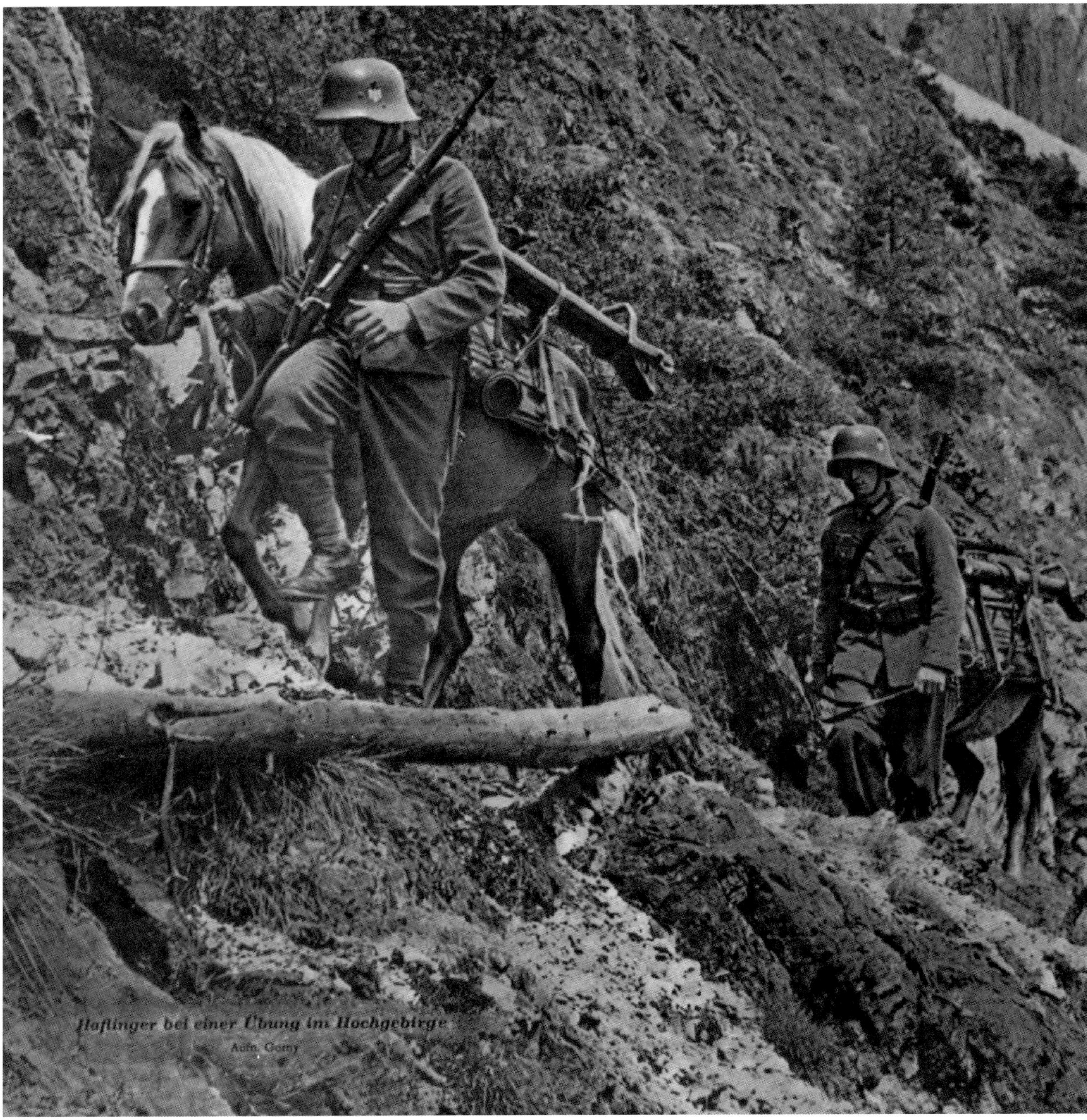

Horses practice in the high mountain region.

Mountain horses and mules take heavy loads from the mountain infantrymen.

The bugler corps of the Army Riding and Driving School at Krampnitz were all mounted on white horses.

Captured Russian soldiers and civilians were pressed into service for the unending care of horses.

Bringing water to the "horse collective place."

5

Supply in the Field

I. Forage

Daily forage rations of oats and hay varied according to breed. The oats ration in 1941 (one ration equaled one day's requirements) was five kilograms for cavalry mounts and light draft horses, six and one-half kilograms for heavy draft horses, and eight kilograms for very heavy draft horses. The hay ration varied from four to five kilograms.

A field unit began operations with a forage supply of oats: one ration carried by the horse or his vehicle, one ration on his vehicle, one ration on ration supply train I (horse-drawn), and one ration on ration supply train II (motorized). All horse-drawn vehicles were loaded with one bale of compressed hay.

Because of the transportation difficulties expected to occur in the East, the field forces were directed to utilize local animals, and to obtain forage from the occupied areas. The ease with which forage could be supplemented was overestimated, however, for farm animals in Russia were not regularly fed grain, and few oats were planted. Even green forage and grazing land were rare in large parts of the country, especially in the central and northern fronts.

The rapid German advance in 1941 did not allow time to collect and distribute even what forage could be found. Not until 1942, when the front became stabilized, was the problem of obtaining local forage adequately solved. The situation was made even more serious by the breakdown in rail transportation during the first winter. As an item of lesser importance, forage was transported to the front only in minimum quantities, resulting in an enormous loss of horses.

Describing his experience with forage supply, the then assistant chief of staff of the Ninth Army, and later of Army Group Center, stated as follows:

> Regulations provided that each horse should receive four kilograms of oats and hay daily. It was thought at the beginning of the Eastern Campaign that a large part of the requirements could be taken from the land. At the most it was considered that oats might have to be carried in.
>
> This was hardly the case, for even in such fertile regions as the Ukraine requirements could not be fully met. In the sectors of Army Groups Center and North, characterized by swamps, forests, and steppes, not only oats but, even more important, hay was lacking. In summer and fall green forage offered a partial substitute for oats in the central sector, where horses fed well on grass and clover, and occasionally even on green grain. A mixture of oats and rye, whole or chopped, or rough ground corn, and even black oats to which salt and calcium were added, were eaten without ill effect.
>
> The emergency began with the approach of winter. Horses were soon dying en masse, especially on the central front. There was no forage stockpile then, and the few supply trains that were still running could only carry essentials, primarily ammunition for use against the Russian winter offensive.
>
> Very occasionally some oats and a little preserved fodder would arrive, the latter being especially nutritious, but not in sufficient quantity to warrant mention. The first carload of hay and straw arrived at the beginning of 1942. Ninth Army was forced to issue only a portion of the authorized oats ration, at times only one-half kilogram, and to use roof thatch as green fodder. Hay could not be taken from local farmers, for they too had to keep their animals alive. During the 1941 advance oats were rarely found, and then in negligible amounts.
>
> The reversal before Moscow, and the extreme cold presented endless difficulties. The horse devoured wooden hay racks, thick branches and whole saplings, gnawed at beams and wooden walls, and even consumed sawdust, wood shavings, and cardboard. Thousands of horses died daily of starvation and exhaustion.

Even in the more fertile regions forage requirements could not be fully met. In mid-February 1942, one corps reported that its authorized strength had been maintained by utilizing local farm horses. Only 11 percent of its more than 16,000 horses had had to be assigned to light farm work or be put out of service; 34 percent could be returned to good health in six to eight weeks if given proper care, and 55 percent were still combat worthy. Of the oats ration, 35 percent was requisitioned from the occupied territory, and 45 percent was transported by rail through supply channels. Roof thatch was substituted for coarse fodder, which was not otherwise supplied.

The sole means of alleviating the situation on the central front was to send all animals not absolutely needed to areas where forage was more plentiful. The larger horses were intended for such transfer, but only if their complete recovery could be expected; otherwise they were slaughtered, and the meat used to supplement human rations.

The horse replacements that arrived in late spring of 1942 included animals of divergent qualities. Owing to the continued scarcity of forage, however, the best animals were transferred to pasture for use later in the year.

The number of horses sent to winter quarters was determined by the tactical units, while the supply and administration branch set up the depots and provided forage. Summer hay crops harvested by special details were stockpiled in rear areas. The horse depots also served as resting places for horses enroute to veterinary stations, and particularly to or from the zone of interior.

To increase local farm production, horses requiring rehabilitation were occasionally turned over to the peasants, who provided forage. It was least difficult to feed the local farm horses. They were very frugal eaters, and usually had never been fed oats, being turned loose to graze in the woods and meadows where even pine needles were not unusual fare. One-half kilogram of oats added daily to their diet produced a visible benefit.

In the warm periods of the year it was relatively simple to provide adequate forage. Every opportunity for grazing was fully utilized. Horses that had grown emaciated during the winter soon recovered in the warm sun. Unfortunately, the gnats and horse flies were so thick at times that opportunities for grazing were restricted.

After 1941 hay production was stimulated as much as possible in preparation for winter, and winter quarters with adequate forage stockpiles were established. Concentrated oats and hay were used to the extent they were available. Food bags, while widely used, were apt to rot or crack in the severe cold. Wooden racks wide enough for two horses were a good substitute. Horses were seldom fed forage from the ground.

Good drinking water was always available, even though requirements were unusually high, especially during the 1941 offensive. No ill effects from water were suffered.

The supply of forage for mountain units must be planned as a long-term procedure, for alpine regions, or such areas as the tundra of northern Norway, will offer little forage. The mules and small horses used by mountain troops are heavy consumers of hay, which is bulky to transport.

II. Shelter

Since shelter is seldom readily available in the field, some type of production should be improvised, for a horse exposed to the elements will expend a considerable amount of energy to compensate for loss of body heat. In summer rest is impeded by insect plagues, especially in marshy, wooded, and river areas. Units not fully aware of the importance of sheltering horses often failed to exploit all possibilities for affording protection, particularly if the men themselves were exhausted.

Farm sheds and storage buildings could often be used as animal shelters. The actual stables were frequently inadequate, for they had been built for the small panye horses. Moreover, many of the stables belonging to the *kolkhozes* and *sovhozes*—the Russian collective and state farms—were infected by local horses suffering from chronic glanders. In extremely cold weather, horses were occasionally even sheltered in houses. Local stables always had to be examined for protruding nails or other sharp objects that could cause injury. Whenever possible, the straw beds in Russian stables were removed, for they were often found to harbor infectious bacteria. Some of the stables were unbelievably filthy. On one occasion, soldiers removed a three foot layer of rotted straw, dung, and debris to find a good stone floor, of which the owners of the stable knew nothing.

Shelter from the wind could be obtained by hitching horses between the houses of a village, or by protecting them with blankets or canvas, or by a wall of underbrush. In summer, such shelter was often preferable to damp, disease infected stables.

Once the front line had become stabilized, houses and farm buildings became particular targets for fire from the ground and air. At those times animals should be dispersed in woods, if possible on dry, sandy ground.

In the following manner, stables housing from 10 to 15 horses can easily be constructed on the south slopes of low hills, or in valleys. Each horse should be allowed space measuring 1.60 by 3.25 meters. Posts 15 to 20 centimeters thick are dug into the hillside to support the roof and sides. These posts are connected laterally by two poles, to which are added wooden feed racks for each horse. Two posts are then added in front, also to support the sides and roof, and on which harnesses may be hung. The roof, constructed of slender poles placed closely together, rests on cross beams secured to the corner posts, and is allowed to protrude over the front. Either shingles, which are available in even the poorer villages, or leaves or pine boughs covered with roofing paper may be used to cover the roof poles. On each side, double walls at least four and one-half to five meters high should be built from poles about 10 centimeters in diameter. These double walls are then filled with soil. As winter sets in, the rear of the stable may be closed off by another wall of poles, although there must be a window at least at every other stall and two doors. Such a stable has a floor area of about five by 20 meters, and a height of at least three meters at the lowest point. The floor should slope six centimeters for every three meters of distance. Slabs of wood, available in the villages, may be used for flooring, and will assure a dry stable. A ditch dug around the stable will drain away rain and melting snow.

Other types of stables can be built, of course, and those dug more deeply in the ground provide good protection against artillery fire. Deep stables, however, may not allow air to circulate freely, and may become too hot, encouraging respiratory illnesses.

In marshy terrain, or during the muddy seasons, of course, stables must be built above ground, just as must combat positions. While this requires more construction, it is justified by the clear necessity for protecting the horses.

While tents may be used as shelters, there is danger that they will not offer sufficient protection against cold, and that in summer their interiors will become unbearably hot.

In many parts of Russia all available straw was needed for forage, and none was left for bedding. The horses usually stood on bare ground, or on wooden poles or planks. Ferns, heather, other foliage, shavings, paper, or sand can at least be used in the rear of stalls. Damp stalls can easily lead to injuries to hoofs, skin, and hair.

Foxholes large enough for horses were effective protection in the combat zone. One foxhole was built large enough for two to three horses, approximately three and one-quarter meters long, from three and one-half to four and one-half meters wide, and one and one-half meters deep. An inclined entrance is built in the rear, and the excavated soil thrown to the front and sides of the hole. It was said that horses soon learned to enter the holes themselves whenever they heard artillery fire.

III. Replacements

There are three ways to replenish the supply of horses: (1.) requisitioning from occupied territory (usually local farm horses); (2.) employing captured horses (largely panye and small Cossack horses, and the excellent Russian artillery horses); and (3.) supplying replacements from the zone of interior.

The requisitioning of horses from occupied territories is a stopgap solution which, if carried very far, can have undesirable economic repercussions. The feelings of the Russian peasant also must not be disregarded, for he loves his horses as much as does the farmer of any other land. Usually it is his most valuable possession. The requisitioning of pregnant mares, those that have not yet weaned their foals, and horses under four years old should be prohibited. All requisitioned and captured horses should be examined for disease before being placed among the regular teams.

When a large number of horses were captured, they were collected in division or army horse depots, examined, classified, and finally distributed according to need.

The systematic supplying of horse replacements from the zone of interior is the responsibility of the veterinary officers of higher headquarters.

Each mounted and horse-drawn unit included in its combat train a small reserve of horses. In the infantry divisions, the horse reserve was supervised by the supply section of the veterinary companies. In 1939, the reserve for the 5000 horses of a division comprised 35 cavalry mounts and eight light and 15 heavy draft horses. These numbers were insufficient for conditions in Russia, and should have been increased at least 30 percent. From time to time the reserve was supplemented by replacements, usually brought in by truck or rail. Long distance marches were avoided whenever possible, for they involved the expenditure of both time and energy, and usually were conducted under great difficulties. With the breakdown of rail support, however, the High Command decided to have thousands of horses driven to the Eastern Front in order to replace the large numbers that died during the first winter. In some cases, the march involved distances of over 1000 kilometers.

Although contrary to German Army regulations, experience showed that horse replacements should be sent to the front directly from the zone of interior, for army horse depots were too often breeding grounds for infectious diseases. Inspection in such depots was nearly always lax, owing to the shortage of personnel.

It proved very effective to join the horse replacement convoys to the personnel replacement sections of the mounted and horse-drawn units, so that each man in the replacement section could care for one or two horses while enroute. Each horse was equipped at least with a bit, march halter, saddle blanket, surcingle, and feedbag; every other horse with a saddle; and every fourth horse with a complete breast harness with traces.

Replacement convoys carried with them extra horseshoes, nails, grooming utensils, and similar equipment. All replacements should be rested before their assignment to the field forces, although in practice this was seldom done.

Pack animal replacements were trained in the zone of interior prior to their assignment. Full understanding of the many problems involved in supplying replacements in Russia can only come with first-hand experience. The veterinary officers responsible for replacement supply had no difficulty getting such experience, for they were constantly faced with new situations, and often even found themselves in combat side-by-side with the line officers.

At a crossing at the bend in the river Don, Russian prisoners watch the continual flow of supplies. The wagons in the center of the picture are hauling hay.

Bringing in fodder for the horses. A typical infantry division prior to 1944 had 15,500 men, 942 motor vehicles, 1,133 horse-drawn vehicles, and 5,375 horses. Later in the war the number of men decreased to 9,069 and motor vehicles to 615, but due to the lack of fuel the horse-drawn wagons increased to 1,466. Due to the lack of remounts, the horses available to pull the wagons fell to 4,462. Imagine the logistics of providing 53 tons of hay per day to feed the horses of an Infantry division. Reference: United Sates War Department Technical Manual 15 March 1945 TM-E 30-451.

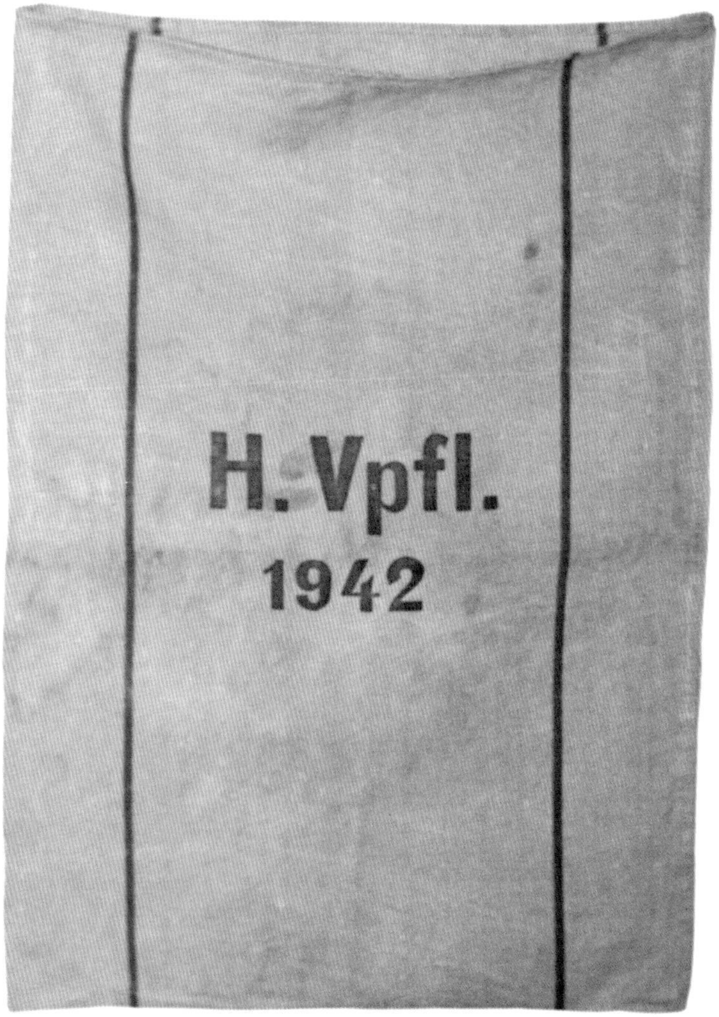

Above: Grain bag for fodder was also used to carry rations such as bread and a variety of other items. *H.Vpfl.* symbolizes "Army Rations Distributing Point." These bags are approximately 28"x40". Below: Soldiers posing for a photo at the stable. They are taking feed from a grain bag marked "Army Rations Distributing Point 1939" and filling individual feedbags.

Fodder for the horses was as important as gas for the vehicles and food for the troops.

Wooden feedbox used to feed two horses at a time of a four-horse team. This wooden feedbox was usually carried hanging from the rear axle of the wagon. Notice the horse eating out of a feedbag like the one pictured in the next photo.

This photo shows the feedbag.

A cotton feedbag also used to feed the horses. Each rider carried one of these. The bags were durable enough to hold water when new.

Men and horses from an artillery battery stopping for lunch.

"With each rest, the first concern is for the horses." - cavalry standard procedure.

"At the Village Well."

6

The Veterinary Service

At the head of the Army Veterinary Service was the Veterinarian General of the Army High Command, who received his technical directives from the Chief Veterinary Inspector of the Replacement Training Army, and his military directives from the Chief of Army Supply and Administration. The Veterinarian General proposed to the latter the employment of the veterinary troops within the army groups and armies. The veterinary units included clinics, horse depots, veterinary depots, mobile research stations, and horse transport columns. In the order of battle, the veterinary companies were organic parts of the infantry divisions.

The veterinary officers on the staffs of army groups, armies, corps, and divisions were subordinate to the Veterinarian General for technical direction, but to their immediate unit commander for tactical purposes. The veterinary officers belonged to the supply echelon of their respective headquarters. Tactical and technical instructions to veterinary personnel were issued as "special directives." Each horse-drawn unit had its own unit veterinary officer.

Veterinary troops were commanded by veterinary officers, except in the case of horse transport columns, which were commanded by line officers assigned to a senior supervising veterinary officer.[4] Veterinary officers, however, retained command over horseshoe personnel of their own units in technical matters.

Toward the end of 1944, the veterinary companies of the infantry divisions were combined with the administrative and medical services into the administrative battalions of the new supply regiments. This measure was occasioned by the shortage of personnel and motor vehicles, and is probably not advisable under normal conditions. It may be, however, that the veterinary officers were better placed within a service unit than a line company, for they were largely reservists with little general military knowledge or training.

Just as a farmer calls a veterinarian only in more serious cases, an experienced column leader or driver was able to diagnose and prescribe treatment for many minor ailments. Losses can be limited if the driver knows his animal and gives it proper care, examining it for sores and wounds at every halt, and readjusting the harness to prevent excessive chafing. If possible, tired horses were led by hand. Horses suspected of infectious diseases were kept separate, and brought to the veterinary officer for examination.

The assignment of non-veterinary officers to supervise the training and care of horses in division and higher headquarters was often viewed by veterinary officers as an unjustified interference with their own functions. This was hardly the case, however, for the veterinarians were properly concerned only with the health and medical treatment of horses, while non-veterinarians were charged with the handling of horses, care of accompanying equipment, and training in horsemanship. Even though these two missions may have overlapped, divided authority was still justified by the fact that the fighting personnel were almost never given sufficient instruction in horsemanship during the war. With its limited facilities, the veterinary service could never have been given responsibility for all aspects of training. Moreover, the field expertise of most veterinary officers was far too limited to permit them an understanding of training requirements.

HORSES IN THE GERMAN ARMY

ZONE OF INTERIOR	ARMY GROUP	ARMY	DIVISION
Veterinary Hospitals Remount Depots Veterinary Depots	One or two army group veterinary hospitals	<u>Installations</u>: two army veterinary hospitals, partially motorized; one army veterinary park, motorized; two horse transport columns, motorized--one horse transport company as of autumn, 1943; one army remount depot; one to two mobile veterinary stations, motorized. <u>Army Veterinary Clinics</u>: Organization similar but larger than veterinary company, without supply section but with horse transport motor trucks. Authorized capacity of 550 horses but often increaased in the East to 2,000 or 3,000 horses; reinforced by voluntary auxiliaries and prisoners of ware. During advance, hospitals moved forward alternately; during combat or position warfare, see below. <u>Army Remount Depots</u>: Authorized capacity of 500 remounts, usually many more; supplemented from the zone of interior, recuperated horses from hospitals, and captured horses. <u>Army Veterinary Depots</u>: Although motorized, is dependent on rail transportation because of 500 tons of equipment including medical and dressing equipment, instruments, horseshoeing equipment, cleats, and gas protective equipment. <u>Veterinary Test Stations</u>: Well-equipped, mobile laboratory for all bacteriological, serological and chemical testing. Tests foods of animal origin from the butcher companies, tests fodder, and systematically tests all army horses for glanders. <u>Horse Transport Column or Horse Transport Company</u>: For employment see below.	Authorized one veterinary company per infantry, mountain or Luftwaffe field division and two veterinary companices per calvalry division. <u>Veterinary Company until 1943</u>: 233 men, two horse-drawn and six motorized transport vehicles. <u>Organization</u>: One command section, one collecting section, one hospital section, one supply section, one rations section. <u>Equipment</u>: Excellently equipped with instruments, x-ray and portable motor-driven dynamos. <u>Mission</u>: Transfer sick and injured horses from combat areas; treat simple cases in hospital section; for others see below. Advances with the supply troops. Assigned to the administrative forces and not to veterinary units, but received technical instructions from the latter and were commanded by veterinary officers. <u>Butcher Company</u>: One per division, fifty men; provided fresh meat and sausages for 19,200 men; protected the unit against trichina and bladder worms.

VETERINARY SERVICES

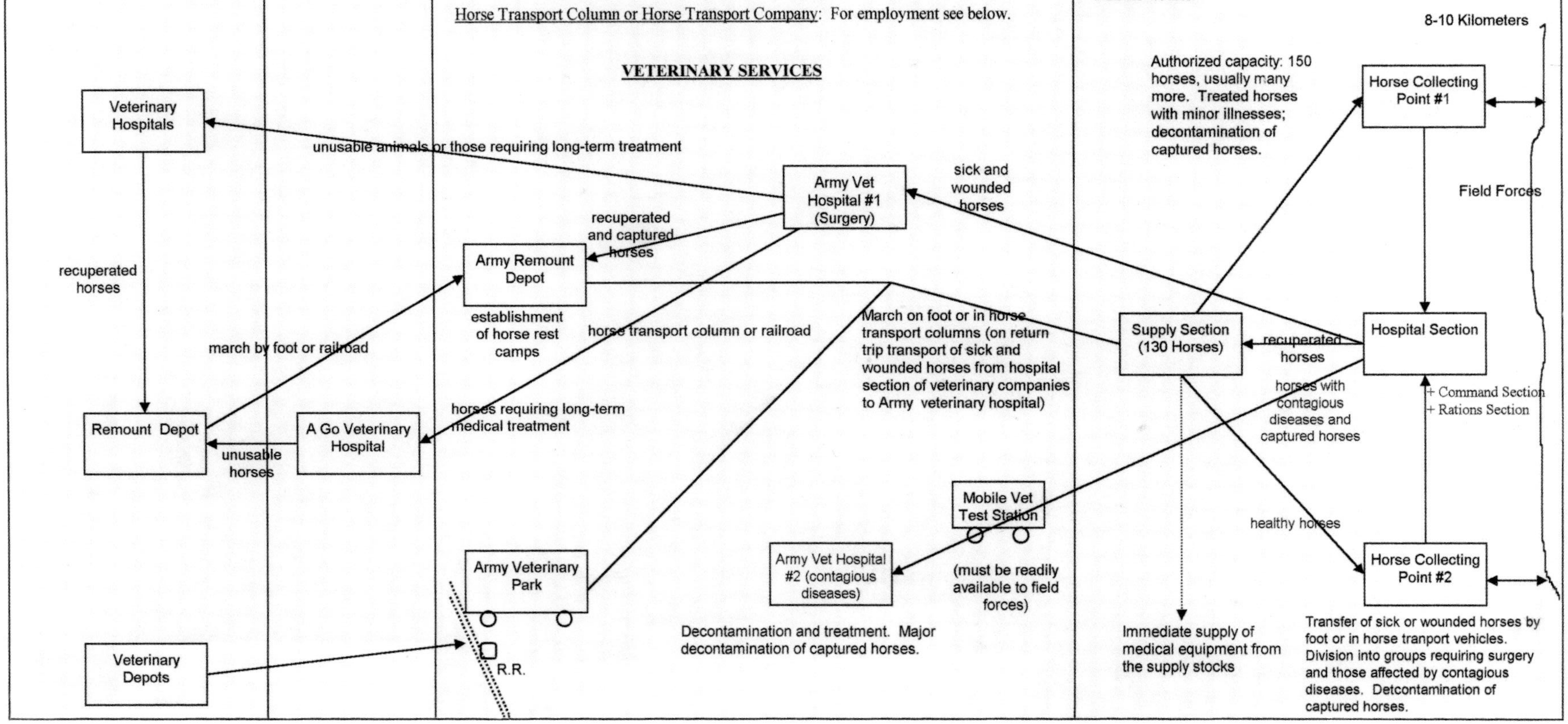

Curt Schulze, Veterinarian General of the Army High Command.

General Schulze was in charge of all veterinarian services of the armed forces from 1938 until war's end. During the war, he was responsible for 1,250,000 horses, 37,000 blacksmiths and 125,000 soldiers. The veterinary service was divided into 236 veterinary companies, 48 veterinary hospitals, and 68 horse transport divisions. The veterinary hospitals treated approximately 100,000 horses daily. After treatment, 70-75% of the horses were able to return to active duty.

General Schulze on one of his many inspection tours.

Colonel (Veterinarian) Dr. Herter, chief of staff of General Schulze.

The man standing by his 1936 model 326 BMW is General Schulze's personal photographer. The markings on the fender stand for Army Group Model.

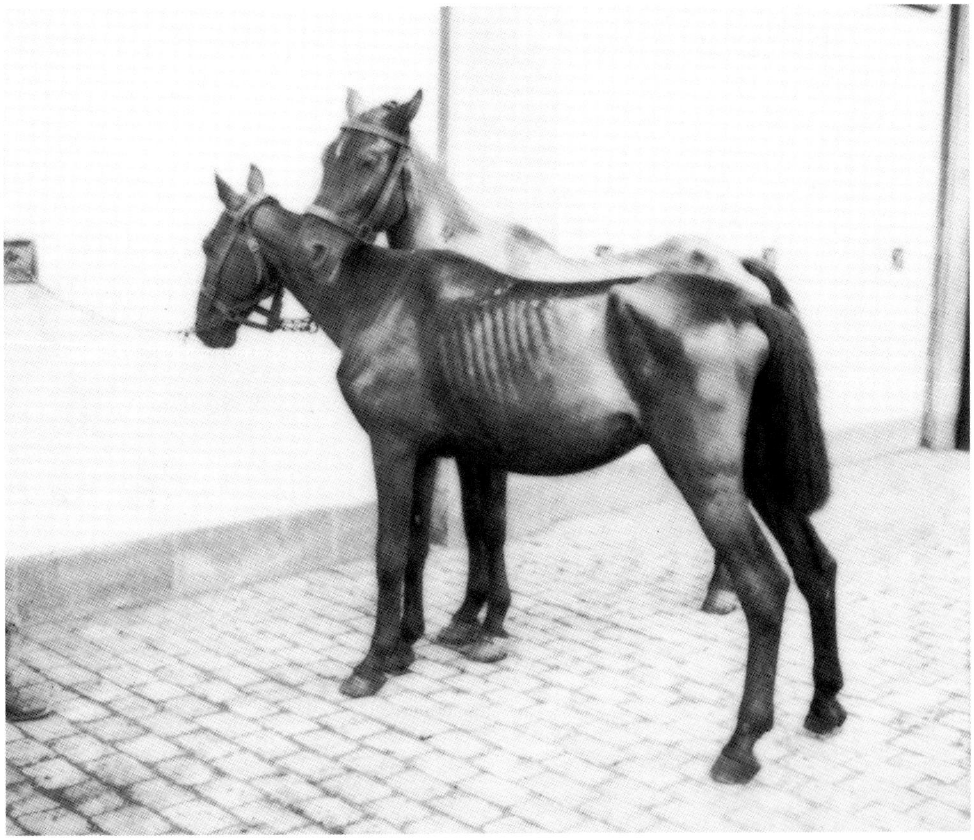

Injured horses awaiting treating.

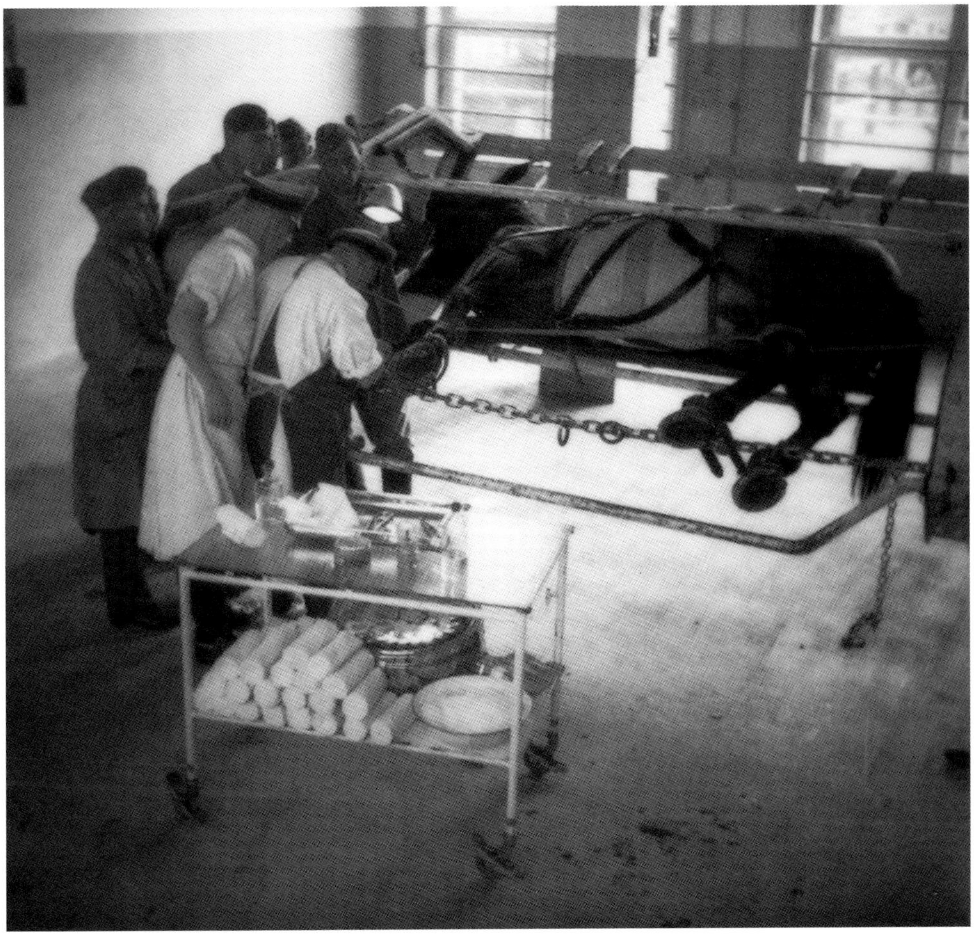

Horse operating table.

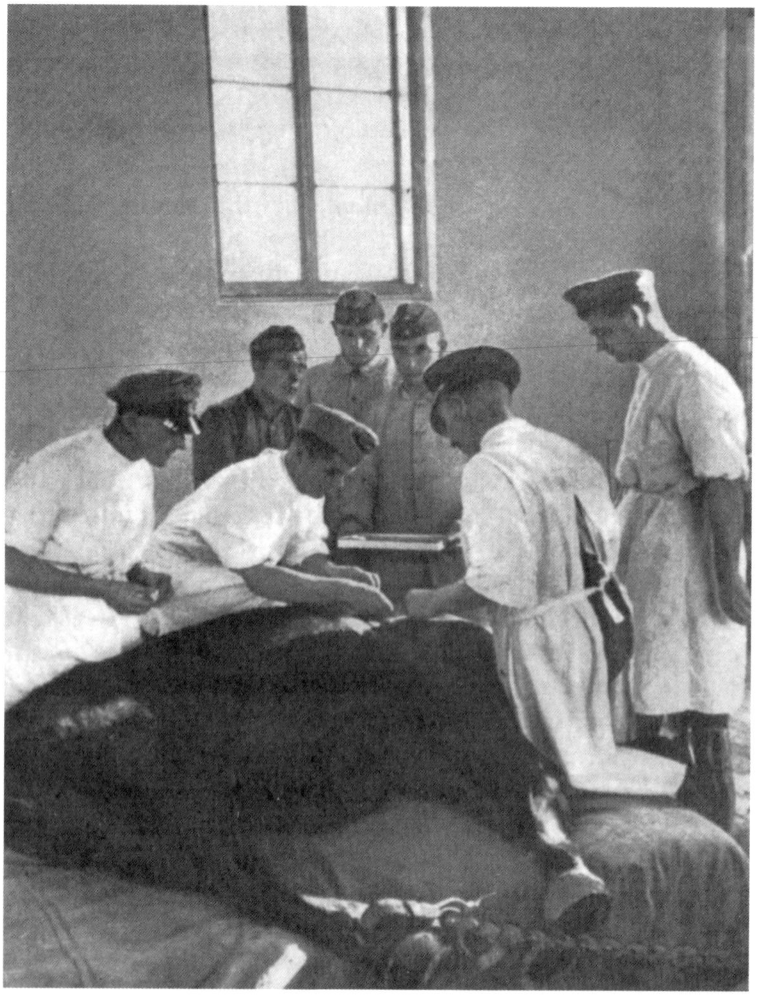

Operation.

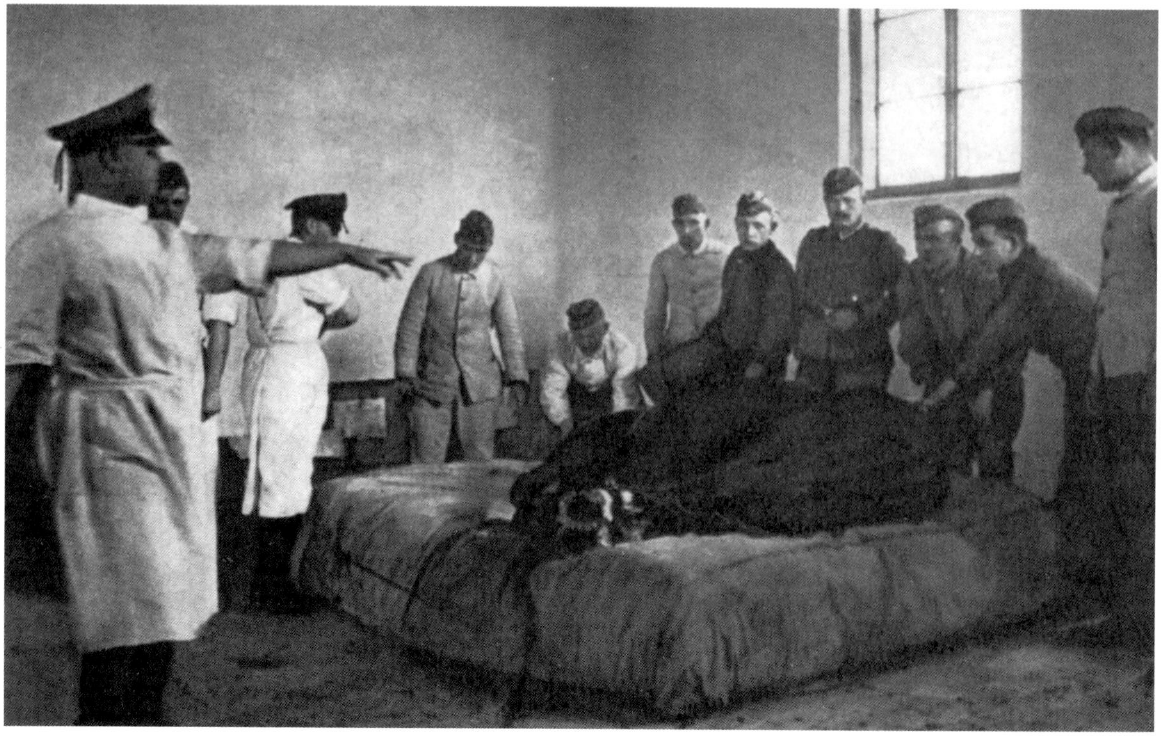

Bed rest.

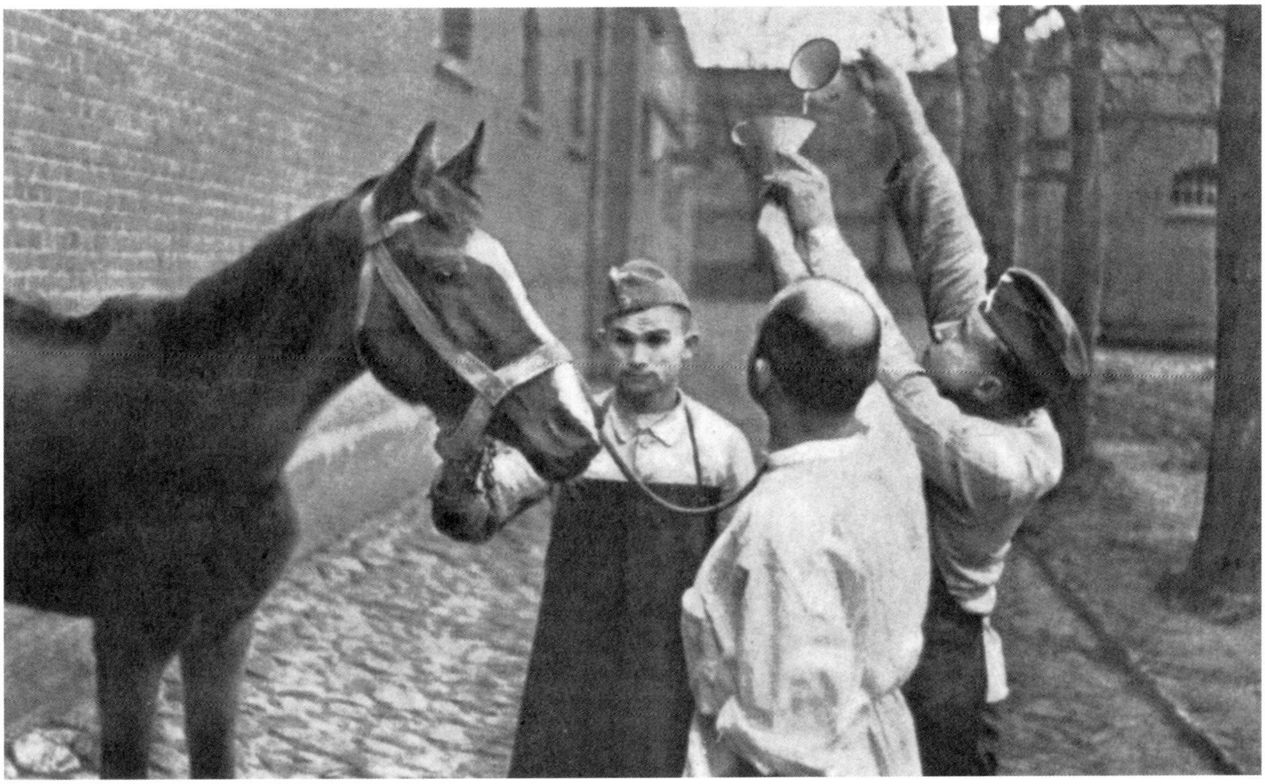

Take your medicine, and you're as good as new, sometimes.

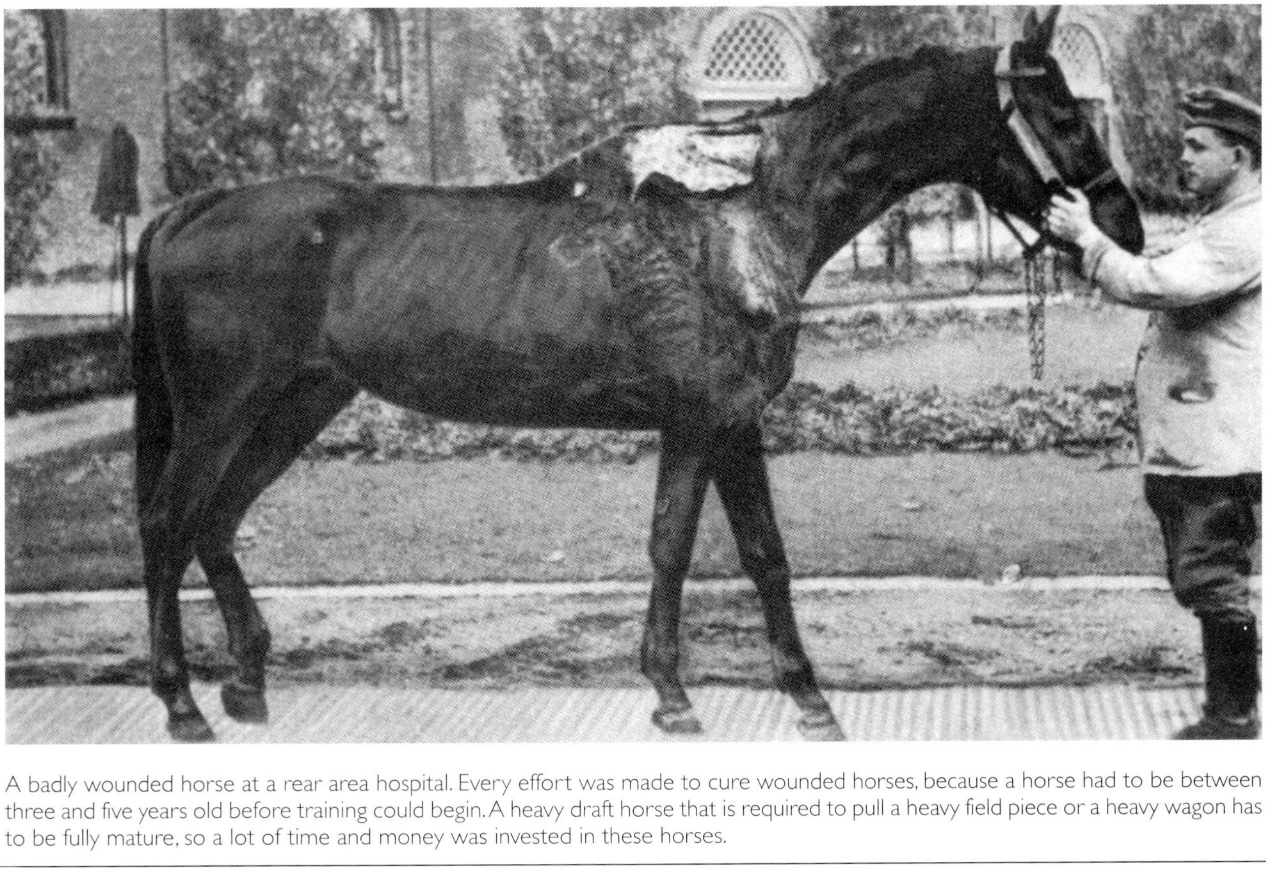

A badly wounded horse at a rear area hospital. Every effort was made to cure wounded horses, because a horse had to be between three and five years old before training could begin. A heavy draft horse that is required to pull a heavy field piece or a heavy wagon has to be fully mature, so a lot of time and money was invested in these horses.

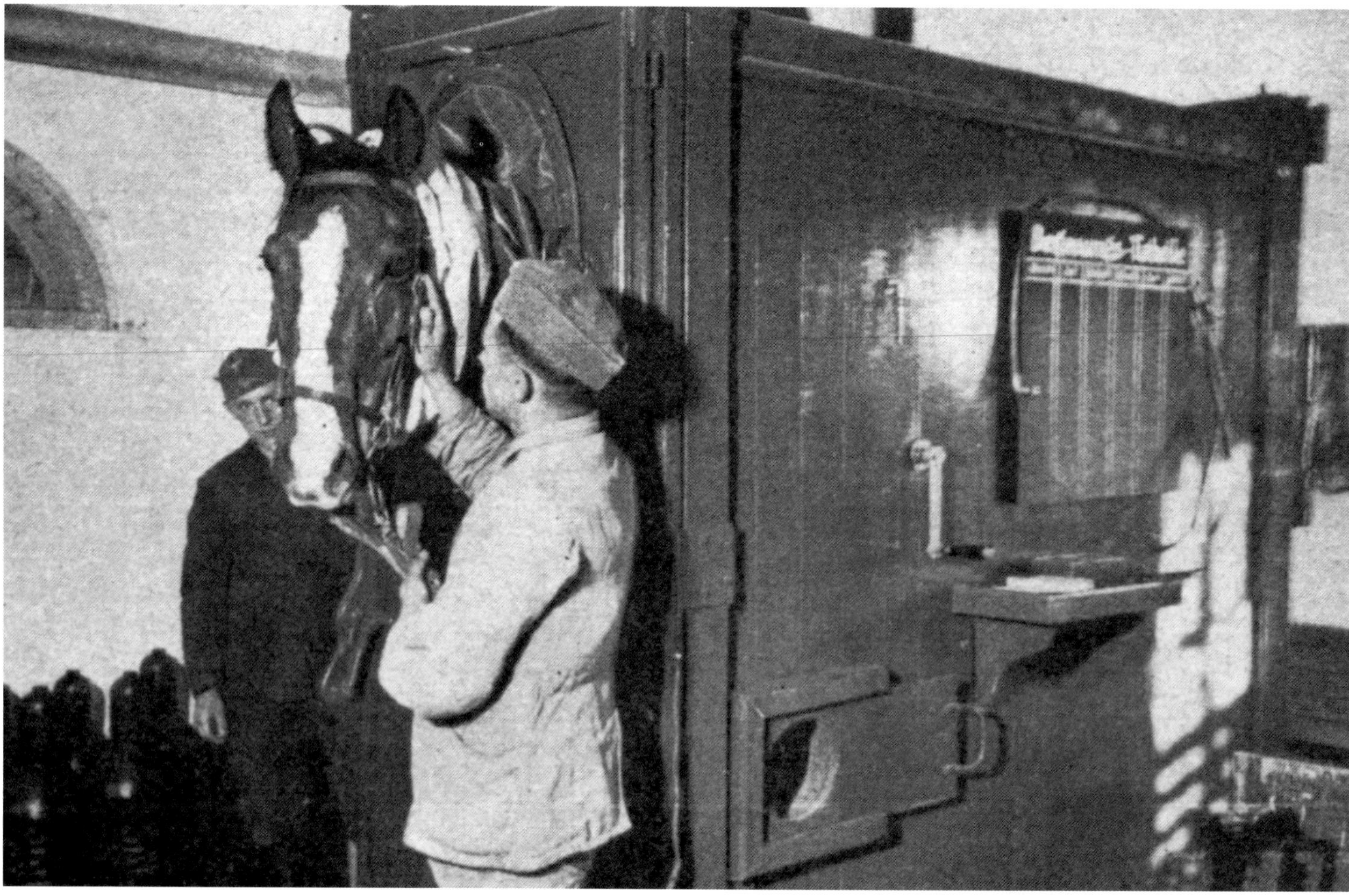

Baths used either gas or steam to rid horses of a variety of infestations. In the lower left corner of the photo you can see the gas cylinders.

To make the life of this horse a little easier, he is getting a steam bath to rid him of infestations.

Inspecting grain at a hospital for horses.

7

The Remount System

I. Procurement

The local breeding of horses to satisfy military demands is economically of great importance, for the purchase of large numbers of horses from foreign sources is very costly. While the horse market can supply the relatively constant number of military horses needed in peacetime, requirements during war increase rapidly, so that Germany was forced to depend upon horses employed commercially within the Reich.

To the extent that this is necessary, horses used in the civilian economy must be suitable for military purposes. The state, therefore, should influence horse breeding accordingly. Government-owned stud farms were established in Germany to assure selective breeding over a long period, and to develop horses suitable for the requirements of both the army and the peacetime economy.

II. In Peacetime

Before the war, purchases within Germany were made by remount commissions, which bought young horses at especially organized remount markets. Purchases were authorized by the Inspectorate of Riding and Driving of the Army High Command. Procurement orders denoting number of type of horses were issued by the inspectorate, which was responsible for the overall management of horses in the Army. The horses were divided into classifications according to probable type of employment.

The three-year-olds purchased by the remount commissions were first collected in remount depots run by the Army. There the Inspectorate of Riding and Driving could survey the entire herd, at the same time checking on the activity of the commission. The young horses, not yet fully grown, grew strong under uniform treatment during their year in the remount depots, and progressed in a common direction even before their actual training began. At the end of the year the horses were transferred either to the services, which conducted their own training, the artillery and cavalry, or to the *Wehrkreis* Riding and Driving Schools, where they were trained to serve in the infantry and other arms.

III. In Wartime

Special measures were required to meet the suddenly increased demand for military horses following the outbreak of war. In 1939, the number of horses in the German Army increased almost in one stroke from 120,000 to 590,000. Throughout the course of the war a large reserve of horses was continually required, many times over the number needed in peacetime.

It was possible to meet the increased demand for horses at the beginning of the war only because all horses in Germany had already been listed according to suitability, availability, and need, a task performed by the Inspectorate of Conscription and Recruiting and its various agencies. Both military and civilian agencies, especially agricultural organizations, collaborated in drawing up lists of horses, in order that consideration could be given to both economic and breeding requirements. Horses could be declared indispensable, just as could persons who held important civilian jobs. Without this careful preliminary work, the sudden induction of thousands of horses would have been hard felt by the national economy.

As the war progressed, the continued high demand for more horses could not be filled by the old system, except by cutting into the stocks of full-grown horses. The number of horses requisitioned in Germany and the occupied territories was in 1940: 148,000; 1941: 282,000; 1942: 400,000; and 1943: 380,000.

At the beginning of the Russian Campaign, not only did the demand greatly increase, but also far more care had to be exercised in requisitioning horses. Mistakes were of course unavoidable: overage or immature horses were too frequently accepted; too large horses should never have been taken; and the induction of valuable studs was especially unfortunate. At the front many mistakes were also made, which in turn added to the strain on sources of procurement. Horses suffering from overexertion were seldom evacuated to the zone of interior while still able to perform light farm work, even though at the front they only burdened the veterinary service, and after recovery and reassignment soon broke down again. Collecting depots and stables were notorious sources of infection, owing to lack of care and adequate supervision.

IV. Procurement in Occupied Territories

Horses were requisitioned from occupied territories in accordance with the same principles applicable in the zone of interior, for the preservation of economic life, especially in agriculture, was to the interest of the occupiers. A considerate policy was especially important in the densely populated nations of Central and Western Europe, where the agricultural economics are sensitive and highly developed. The particular manner in which horses were requisitioned depended on conditions in the respective country, although when possible existing agencies and markets were utilized.

Conditions are different in Eastern Europe, where the sparser population, less developed economics, and hardier breeds of horses made requisition easier. But even here care had to be taken not to damage the local economy, especially since the strength of the partisan movement fluctuated with the kind of treatment extended by the occupiers.

Very few breeds of horses common in other countries were encountered in Russia, where the panye horse is almost universally employed. In utilizing panye horses for military purposes, it must be remembered that this small, usually filthy mongrel is not a plaything, or an animal whose use should be left to the discretion of a unit commander or an individual soldier. Only in cases of emergency should individual units be authorized to requisition horses outside of normal channels. There are several reasons why panye horses should be requisitioned and controlled at higher headquarters: (1.) If agricultural areas are deprived of necessary horses crops will suffer, and the population will join the partisans; (2.) troops who are allowed to requisition farm horses and vehicles at will soon attach to themselves a long, unnecessary train, which hampers mobility and endangers discipline; (3.) the distribution of farm horses and vehicles according to actual overall requirements is possible only by a higher headquarters, which is in a position to see the broad picture; and (4.) the unorganized incorporation of panye horses into combat units is likely to spread contagious disease.

The tendency to over-employ panye columns in the German Army was partially checked by giving proper explanations, and by appealing to the understanding of unit commanders.

In practice, horses were requisitioned most efficiently by command agencies, aided by their subordinate units in the field, towns, and other administrative headquarters, and agricultural supervisory and administrative agencies. Horses were obtained in three ways: requisitioning, purchasing, and hiring.

Horses were requisitioned only in exceptional cases, under direction of the division veterinary officer or, in emergencies, of a lower headquarters.

Purchasing was often accomplished through agencies of the military government. Mayors were instructed to present the town military headquarters with a specific number of horses on a designated date, whereupon the purchases were conducted by commissions who paid established standard prices. The purchase horses were then transferred to the division veterinary companies, which after a period of quarantine allocated them to individual units.

Hiring proved to be the best procedure in most cases. The farmer who permanently lost his horse was soon hungry and unable to work. There was already a serious lack of local horses, for the *kolkhoses* used mostly tractors, which the retreating Russians naturally took with them. Consequently, when the Germans expropriated large numbers of horses during 1941-1942, many farmers were forced to join the partisans in order to eat. For this reason it was wise to hire the farmer along with his horse and wagon. He was released during the sowing and harvesting seasons, and nearby units even helped him work his fields if the combat situation permitted. Often this practice was more effective than the use of arms in combating the partisans.

It should not be forgotten that the communist system of the present and the paternalist pattern of the past have accustomed the Russian people to strict control, regardless who is in charge. They are content to be ruled by any authority whom they believe to be just and considerate, even if the controls are severe and demanding.

V. The Present Remount Situation in the German Federal Republic

The outcome of the war has radically changed the situation as concerns the military use of horses in Germany. Formerly the most valuable area for breeding military horses was East Prussia. So far such East Prussian horses present in Western Germany and suitable for breeding purposes have not been collected in a spot adequate to maintain and make use of the valuable characteristics of the breed. Further valuable sources of lightweight, hardy, warm bloods have disappeared with the loss of other regions of Eastern Germany.

The area now controlled by the Federal Republic produces the heavier breeds that, in part, are more susceptible to disease. On the other hand, since cavalry is no longer widely used there is less need for the light warm bloods, while there is a greater need for powerful draft horses. Thus, the situation is not as serious as it might seem.

These photographs demonstrate the quality of horses and training prior to the war. On the back of these photos is written: "Hanover, April 1939."

Horse troops on the exercise field.

An officer taking his morning ride on the streets of Hanover, 1938.

The Remount Committee selecting horses. This committee consisted of experts responsible for the high quality of horses in the German Army, especially at the beginning of the war.

Above and opposite: Remounts being offloaded from trains.

Remount training: Getting the horse to respond to commands from feet and reins while dealing with the distractions from other horses.

Remount training: Getting the horse accustomed to water early in the training.

Remount training: More difficult training—keeping the horse in line in the narrow confines of a ditch.

Climbing on steep hills in sand dunes—a very safe place to practice this exercise.

Practicing entering and exiting water in a single file.

Under the watchful eye of the instructor, who can be seen at bottom of photo, horses practice going down a steep hill.

Practicing water crossings with remounts at driving/riding school.

Water crossing under combat.

The brand on the horse shows that the breed is a Trakehner. This breed came from East Prussia and Poland, and was known for being spirited, brave, and adaptable. It was nearly wiped out in WWII.

During the war, a large part of remount training was conducted by women in riding clubs and in army riding schools.

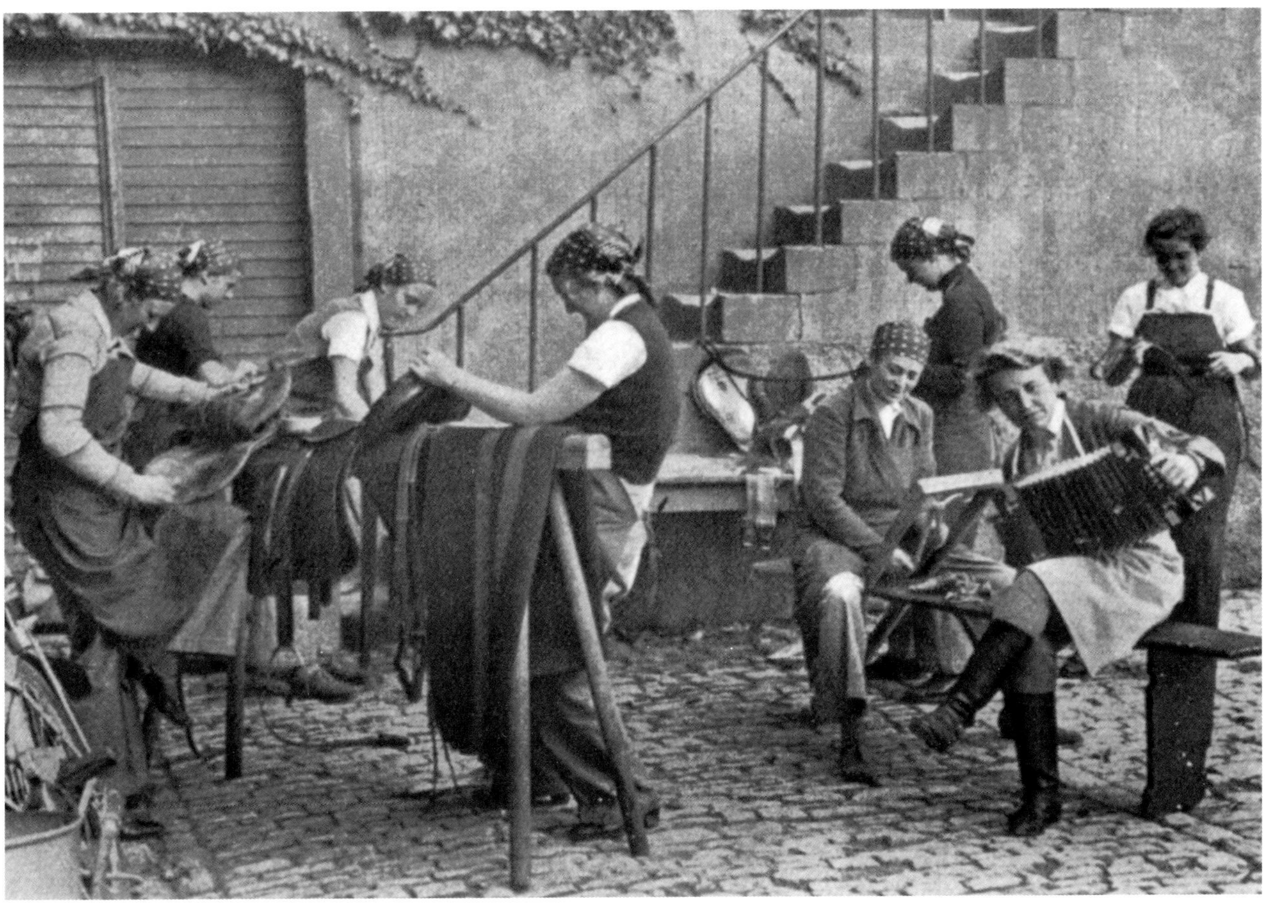

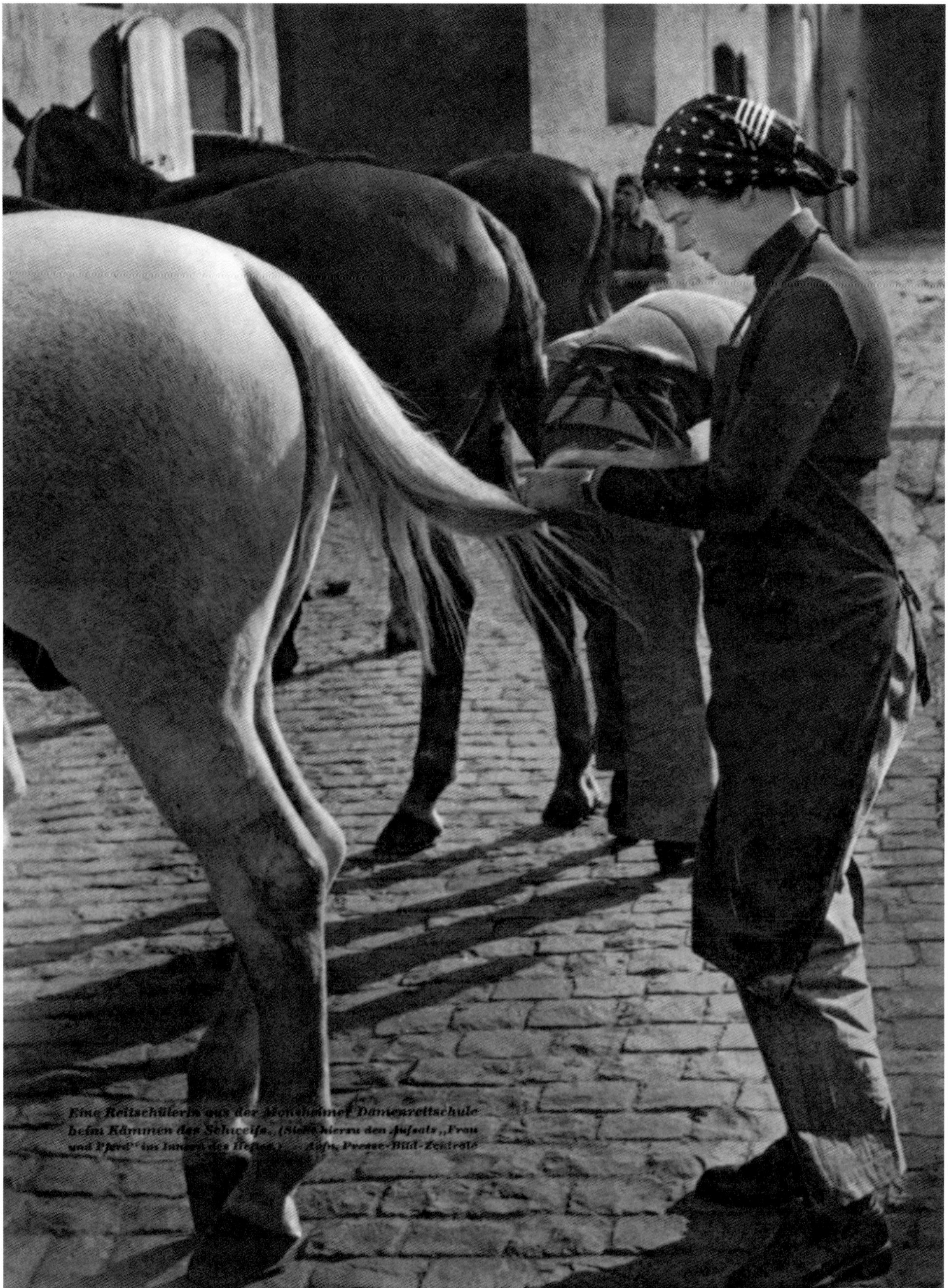

This woman, from the Monsheimer Ladies Riding School, is shown training remounts for the army. Notice the German soldier in the background.

Colonel Stein, inspector for riding and driving for the German Army. He was on the staff of General Schulze.

Above and opposite: Both photos show a veterinary general exercising his mount at a riding hall in France. With the successful conclusion of the French campaign, the German Army gained not only the French Army's stock of horses, but also horse breeding farms in Normandy and riding and remounts facilities.

8

The M1925 Army Saddle

The Model 1925 Army Saddle (also known as the "M25," or the "Army Saddle 25") was the standard army saddle. Saddles of older manufacture were replaced as they became consumed. The Army Saddle 25 came in five sizes. The sizes are stamped on the rear of the saddle on the leather and also on the rear of the tree.

Size Number 1 for narrow-ribbed horses with high withers,
Size Number 2 for narrow-ribbed horses,
Size Number 3 for middle strong horses with high withers,
Size Number 4 for middle strong horses,
Size Number 5 for horses of the large sort.

The (opposite) saddle seat ***a*** lies on the saddle tree, is capped with reinforcing leather ***b*** in the front of the saddle, and a pommel strap ***c*** on each side through the hook ***I*** securing the front of the seat to the tree.

Behind, in the middle of the upper piece of the seat, is found a metal slot ***d*** for the middle pack strap. Underneath ***d*** in the back is usually found the number of the saddle size 1-5.

The saddle skirt ***e*** is fastened with its upper rear pieces under a leather flap with one or sometimes two screws to the tree.

The saddle skirts have knee rolls

f that are filled with felt, the early model saddles do not have the knee rolls. Over the knee pad is a hook ***g*** riveted on to secure the saddle bag strap.

The lining of the knee pads continues over the upper edge of the saddle skirt in an attachment with a notch, through which the buckle strap which is nailed to the tree serves to secure the saddle skirt to the tree.

The saddle pads ***h*** are upholstered with wool. Both pads have a leather shoe in front and behind for the tree to slide into (the front leather shoe stitching is usually lose from the pad from improper storage (laying the saddle on the ground and bending the skirts in and pulling the stitching away from the front shoe. On the back of the saddle are two buckles ***k*** and ***m*** plus the buckle tongue ***l*** they are used for securing equipment.

The laced saddle girth,(see photo)is made of 22 hemp laces and is made in four sizes. The 22 hemp laces are pleated together in the middle of the girth and have two roller buckles in the middle of the pleat.

Stirrup

Stirrups (opposite) are manufactured from steel. They are either painted black or are polished steel (see photo) and are usually letter coded with makers mark and Waffenamt.

They roughened step ***a*** and of the bow ***b***, above which is an eye ***c*** for the stirrup strap. The step ***d*** is shown from the bottom.

Stirrup strap

Stirrup straps (opposite) come in three sizes on one end they have a double buckle and the other end comes to blunt point and has buckle holes that are numbered for adjusting the length of the stirrups.

Note: the leather of the stirrup straps and the leather of the 3 billet straps are attached to the tree. The 3 billet straps on each side is where the two buckles of the girth are attached, leaving one strap as a spare in case of breakage. The girth is numbered to fit three sizes of horses' girths. If the leather of the billet straps is dry rotted, it should be replaced for safety sake if you intend to use the saddle.

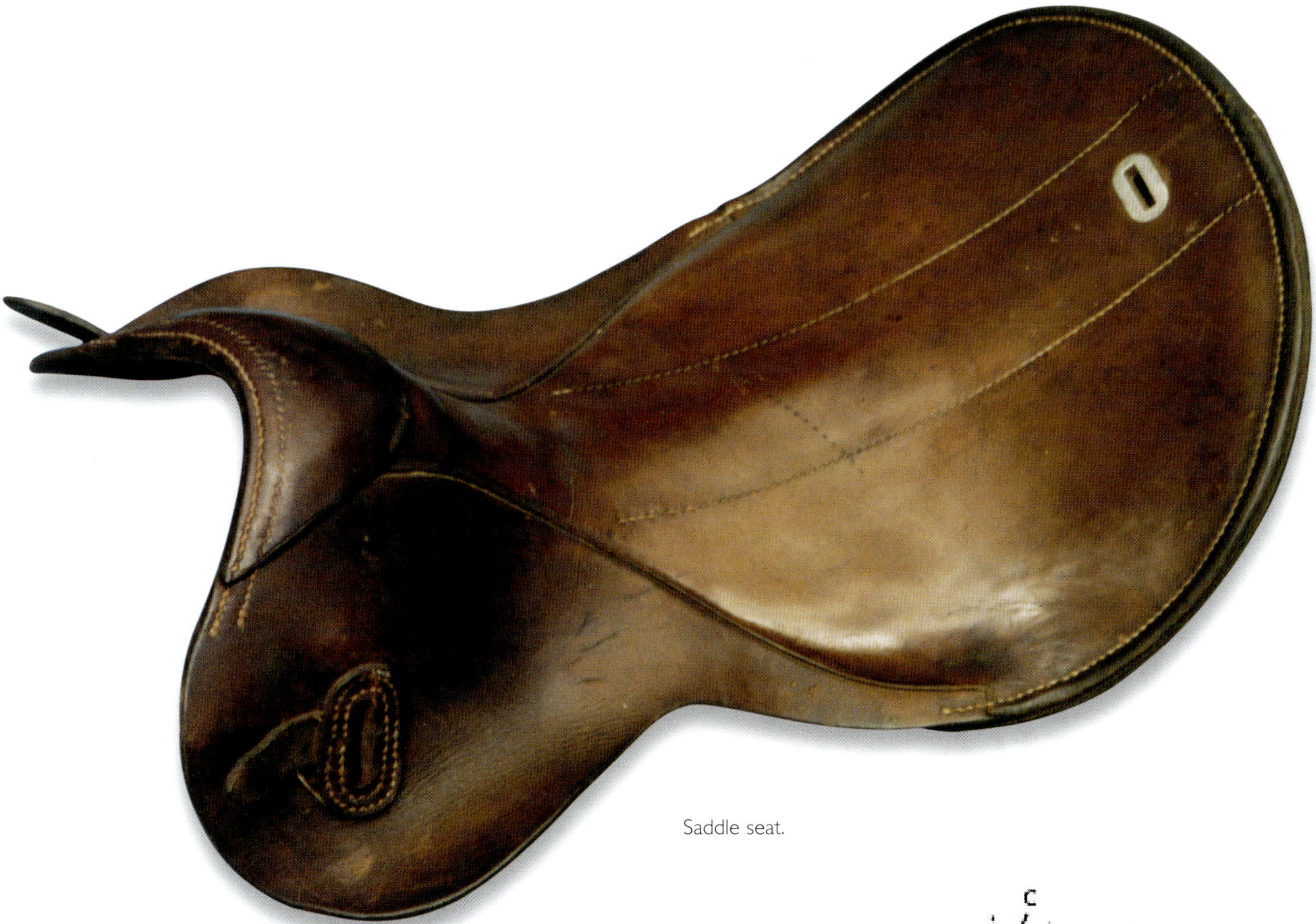

Saddle seat.

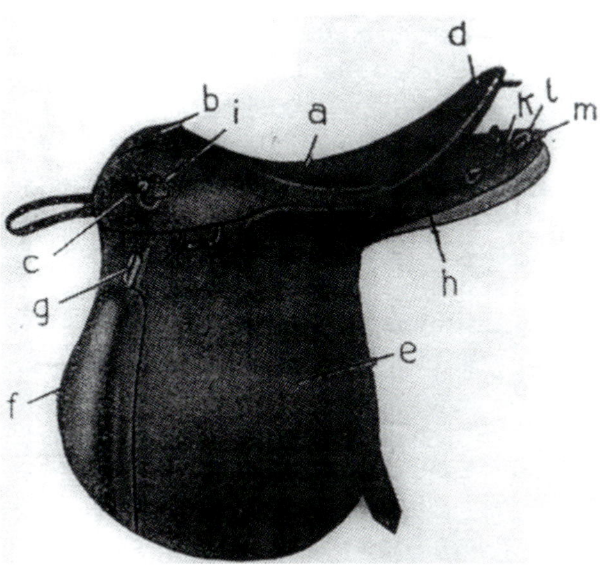

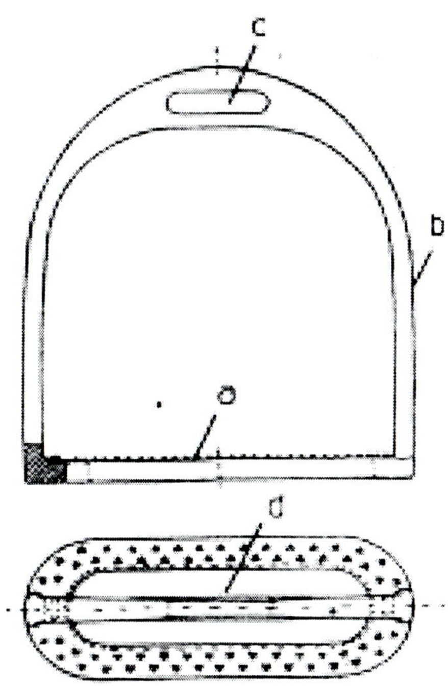

Saddle tree.

Saddle pad (top view).

Saddle pad (reverse side).

Saddle skirts.

Top: A pair of bright steel army stirrups. Bottom: An unmatched pair of steel army stirrups. The one on the left is the same type as the pair above, but is painted black. The stirrup on the bottom right is a bit thinner than the others, and is also painted black. All three variations are marked (*waffenamt*) either on the bottom, or just to the right of the stirrup strap slot.

Standard German Army saddle girth made up of 22 hemp laces. Dated 1942.

This (above) was the older model girth. It consisted of eight strands of off-white cotton strips held in place by three leather keepers. This girth was replaced by the web girth on p89.

Roll call with saddle inspection.

9

Cavalry Equipment

The M34 saddlebags. The left bag was for horse care equipment. The right was for the rider's personal equipment, and could be used as a backpack. Above the saddles is the connecting piece that attaches them. This connecting piece allows the rider to adjust the bags forward or back.

The M40 saddlebags. They were issued in February 1940 in an effort to reduce the amount of equipment and weight. The left bag is for the rider's personal gear (called the "small pack.") The right bag holds the horse care equipment, and was referred to as the "large pack." These bags usally went on the back of the saddle.

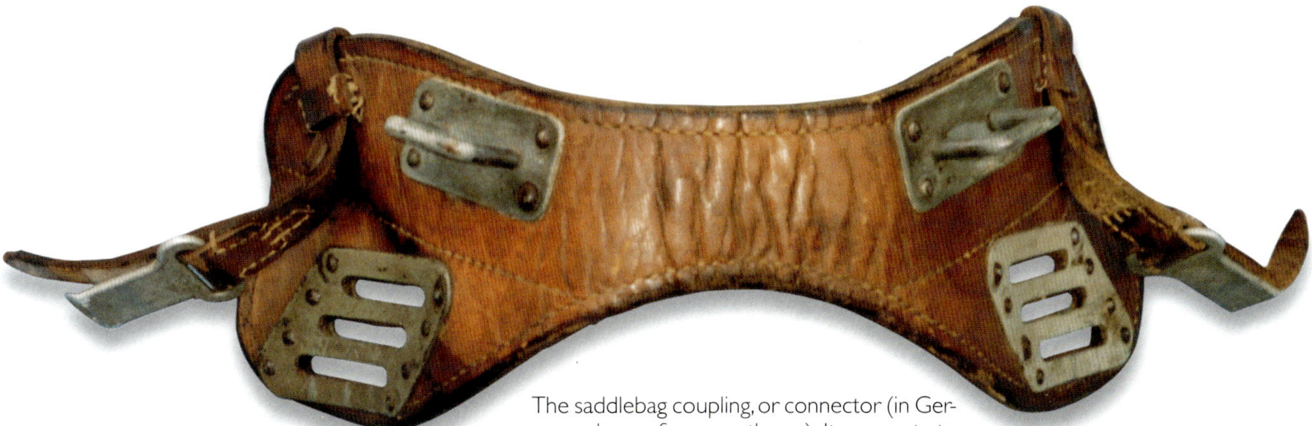

The saddlebag coupling, or connector (in German: *uberwurf*, or overthrow). It connects to the saddle; then the saddlebags are connected to it. This piece is somewhat hard to find.

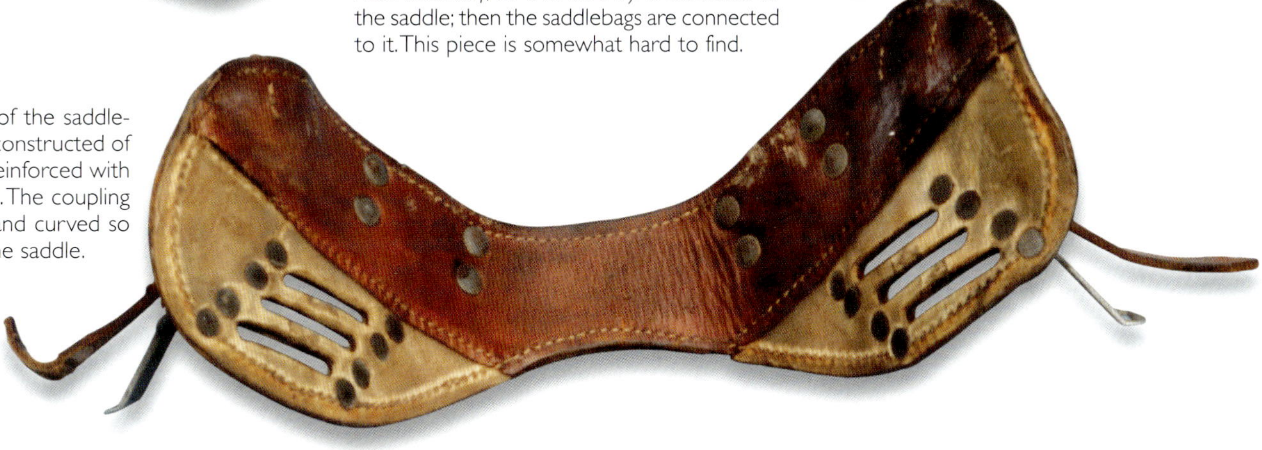

The reverse side of the saddlebag coupling. It is constructed of brown cowhide, reinforced with a layer of rawhide. The coupling is pressed down and curved so it fits flat against the saddle.

Contents of M34 Saddle Bags

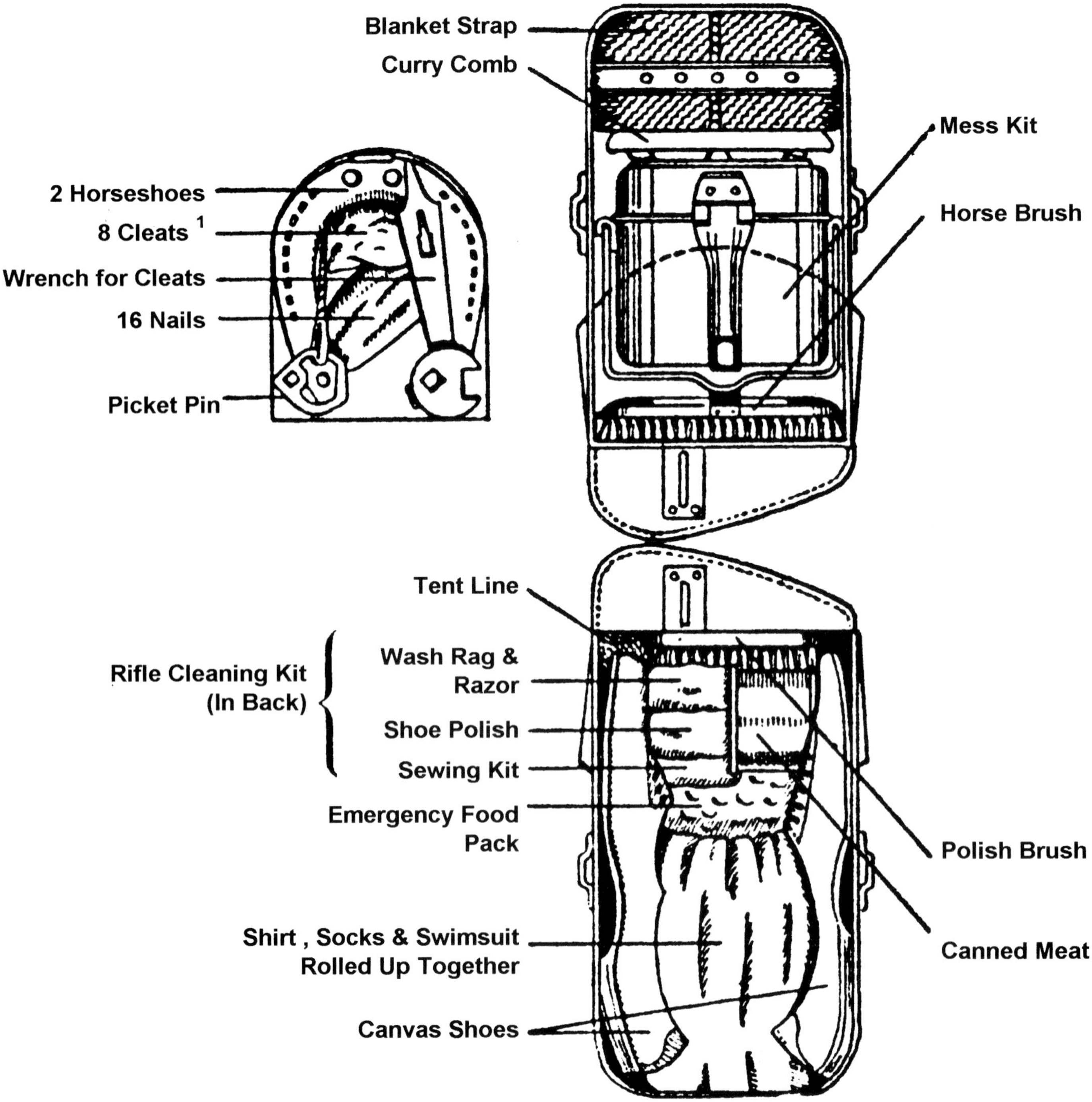

[1] Steel cleats could be screwed into the horseshoe with the cleat wrench for better traction in ice or mud.

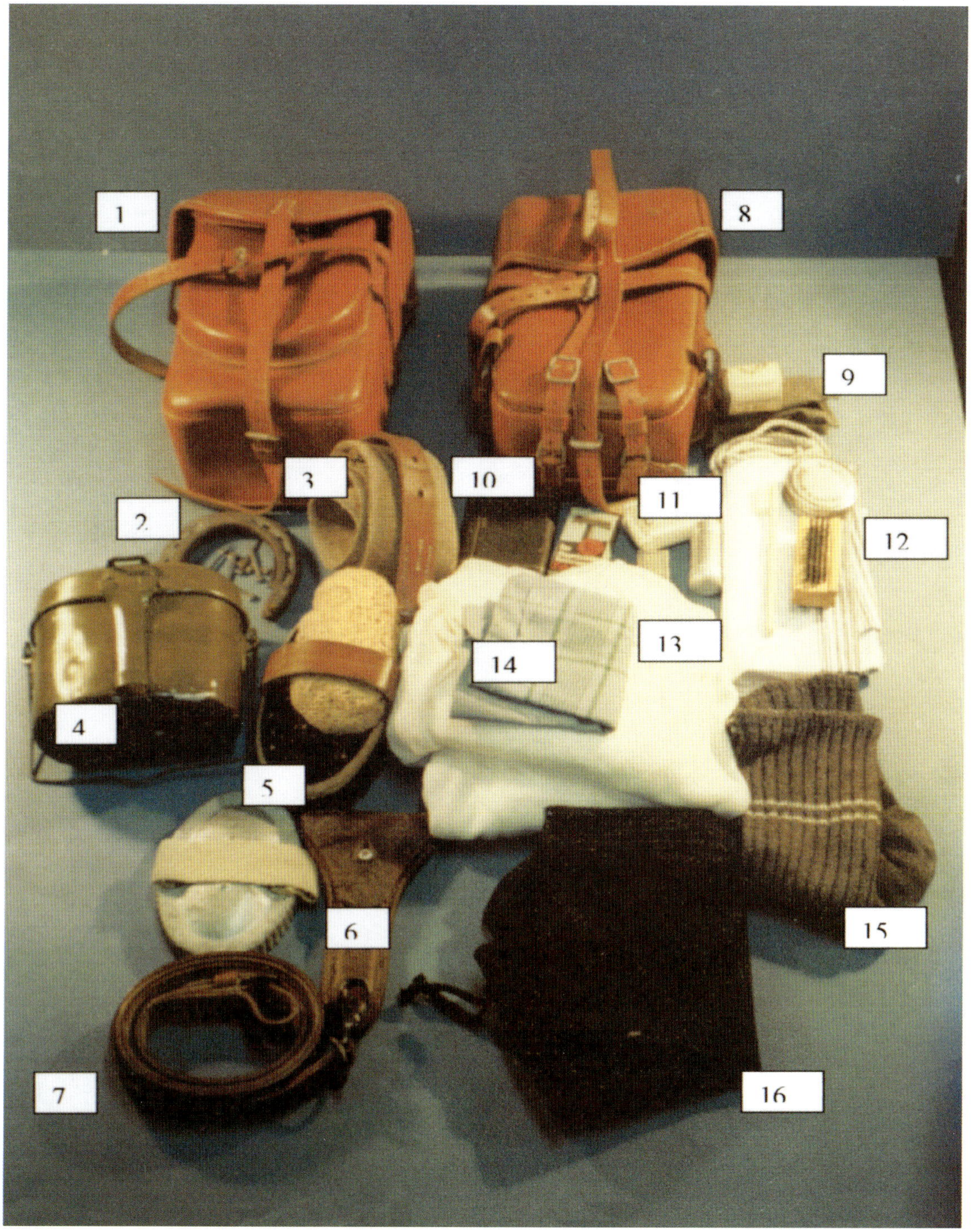

1. M34 left bag for horse care equipment
2. Horseshoes and 8 nails
3. Blanket strap
4. Mess kit
5. Horse brush, sponge, and currycomb
6. Cleat tool
7. Lead line
8. M34 right bag for rider's personal belongings
9. Soap, sewing kit, and tent rope
10. Rifle cleaning kit
11. Razor, blades, and brush
12. Towel, shoepolish, and toothbrush
13. Long underwear
14. Handkerchief
15. Socks
16. Swim trunks

Above and opposite: Two views of the M25 saddle with the M34 saddlebags, mess kit, helmet, blanket, grain/forage bag, and *zeltbahn* (shelter quarter/poncho).

The Model 1940 saddlebag, and some of the items it would carry: spare socks, soap, tent line, matches, needles, thread, handkerchief, Steiner brand pipe tobacco, pocketknife, washcloth, comb, shaving brush, razor, razorblades, toothbrush, and a deck of skat playing cards. It also had pockets for three clips of ammunition.

Model 1940, referred to as the large bag, with some of the items it might carry, such as a mess tin, horse brush, blanket strap, etc.

Contents of the left saddlebag that carried items for the care of the horse.

A large horseshoe for a draft horse, showing the type of cleats that could be screwed into the horseshoe with the cleat wrench for traction on ice. The other end of the cleat wrench could also be used for smaller cleats on smaller horseshoes. It was also used as a small hammer and hoof-pick, and the end was used to clean out the cleat holes.

Two examples of horseshoe wrenches. The one on the right is *waffenamt* but many were not. The issued horse comb, dated 1942, was purchased in Normandy from a farmer that had German horses quartered at his farm. This comb was left behind. The only reason he parted with it was because of the two missing teeth. The Normandy area is horse country and any horse care equipment left by the Germans was used to its utmost.

Issued boot polish and saddle soap that would be important in keeping the leather equipment in good condition.

On the left is a currycomb dated 1943; on the right is a horse brush dated 1941.

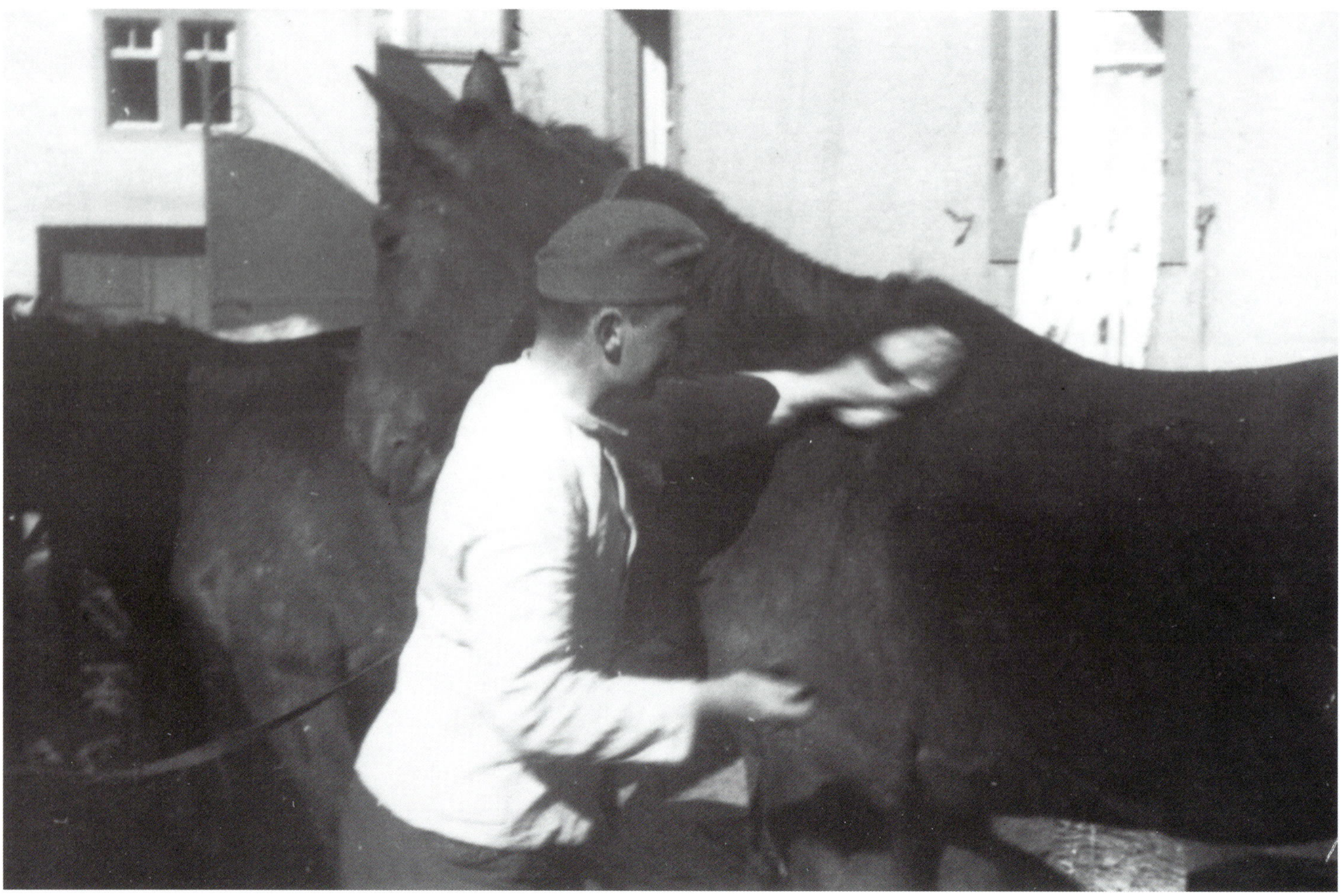

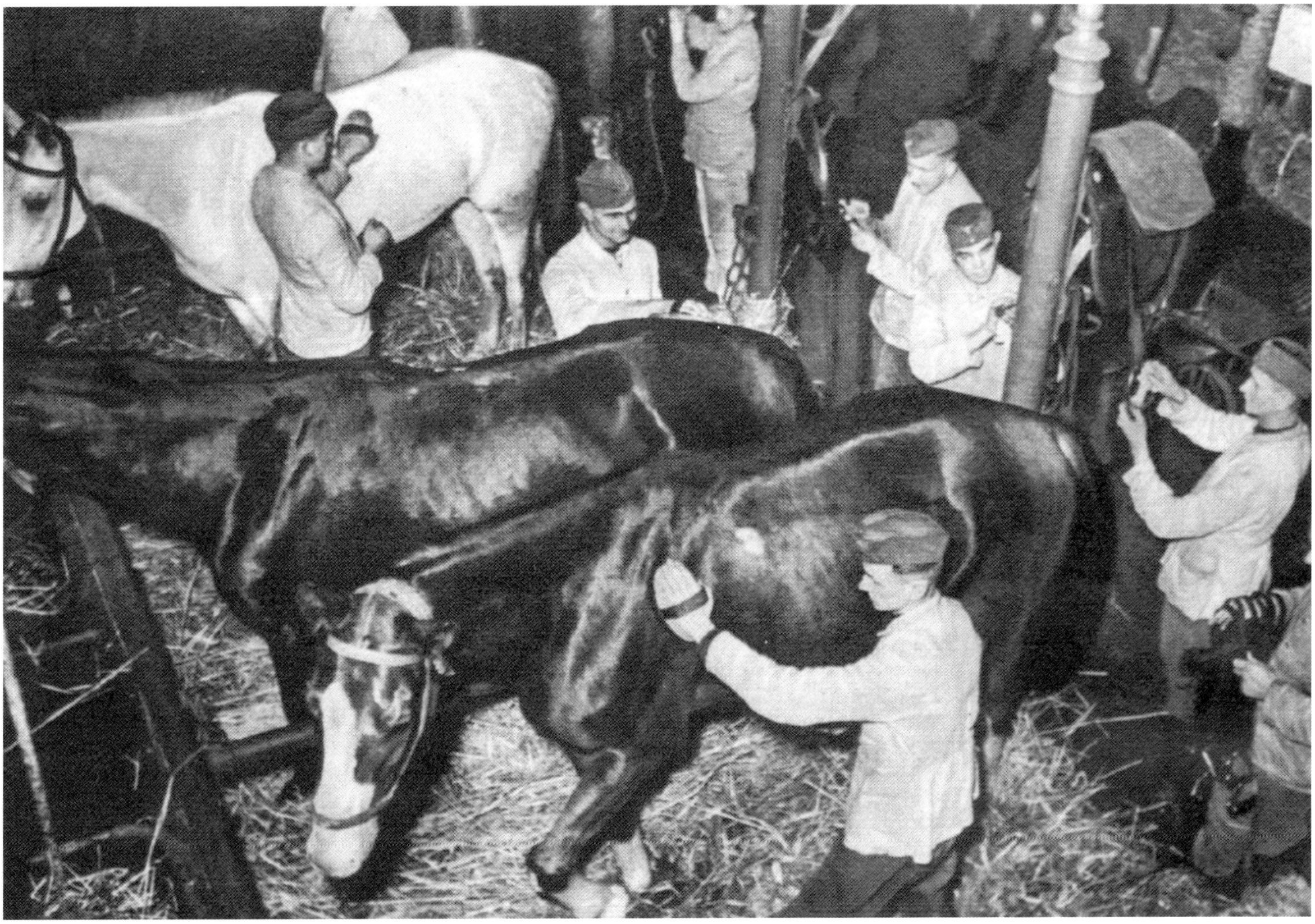

In these photos the soldiers, wearing their white work uniforms are grooming the horses. The large horse brush was used to brush the horse. The currycomb had metal ridges and was used to remove caked on mud and remove the hair on the brush as it built up. The currycomb was not to be used on the horse's legs or other sensitive areas.

The care of the horses was almost constant work.

Stable of the 6th Cavalry Regiment.

The M1940 saddlebag with cavalry boots, picket stake, and trade badges. The first from the left trade badge is for the veterinary service; the others are badges for qualified farriers. The picket pin was used to tie a long rope to, so the horse could graze without being attended. The horse had to be trained so it did not get tangled up in the picket pin rope.

A closer look of the standard issue spur and the leather lip above the heel, which prevents the spur from slipping down.

Above and opposite: The three most common bits used by the German Army in WWII. Left is the straight bar bit that was gradually replaced by the S bit in the middle; the watering bit on the right was used in conjunction with the S bit. The watering bit was used for more passive activities while the S bit with its moderate port was used for more immediate commands. (The bend in the middle bar that presses against the roof of the horse's mouth is called the port.) The higher the port, the harsher it is on the horse's mouth. The S bit was not considered by horse experts of the era to be a harsh bit.

A field-made pad to be attached to girth made from strips of cloth for padding and *zeltbahn* (shelter quarter/poncho). Apparently a soldier tried to make his horse's load a little more bearable.

The pad attached to a girth.

At right: Ammunition supporting straps for mounted personnel. They did not have D rings for attaching a pack.

Standard cavalry supporting straps ("Y") straps without D rings.

Medical pouch for mounted personnel.

Same pouch in the open position.

Medical pouch for mounted troops. This pouch mounts on saddle the same as a saddlebag.

Same pouch in the open position.

Blanket strap, carried in the left saddlebag. This was used to hold the blanket on the horse to cool him down. It is occasionally incorrectly called a girth. For safety reasons, no girth would have only one strap/buckle.

The blanket strap in use.

The M1941 Horse Gas Mask. It was constructed of dark brown bakelite cones that were placed up the horse's nostrils. They were held in place by being clipped to the horse's headstall. Filter canisters were screwed into the side of the cones and the air outlet was at the bottom of the cone.

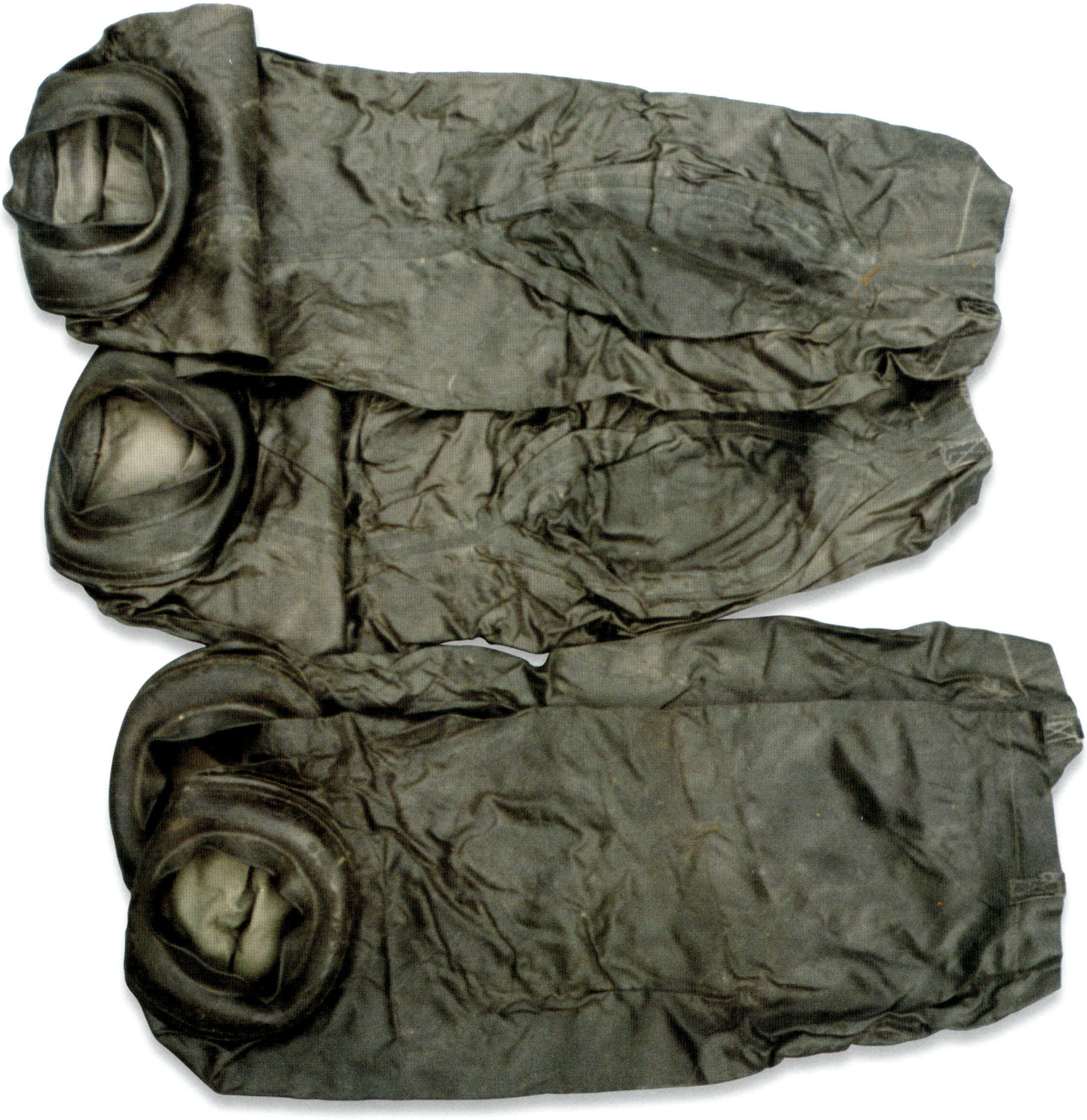

Gas Gaiters. They were used to protect the horse's legs from gas.

A horse gas mask model 1938 dated 1941. The round disk in the foreground is a cardboard protective disk that is to be removed before use.

The canvas carrying case for the horse gas mask.

This rather comical hat was used to protect the horse's ears from insects.

Two examples of horseshoe pouches that were carried by non-saddled draft horses. The pouches were attached to the harness and contained pre-fitted horseshoes. One horseshoe was pre-fitted for the front hoof and one was pre-fitted for the rear hoof. These horseshoes were pre-fitted in case a shoe was lost and a farrier was not handy.

Halter and lead line. The lead line is approximately six feet in length and is marked "L.L.G. Thuringen 1939."

Two pictures of the standard German halter.

This picture shows two cavalrymen wearing M18 helmets and leather seat riding breeches. Hanging down between the horse and the company 1st sergeant is the leather lead line and a good view of the S bit.

Rider's breeches. These breeches with a gray leather seat were issued to all mounted troops regardless of rank. They were full cut in the seat for plenty of room. The leather made for hard wearing and it gave the rider a little more secure seat in the saddle, since it did not slip as easily as a cloth seat.

The helmet-carrying strap that was used to carry the helmet on the saddle when not in use. This strap also carried helmets on the outside of vehicles.

Another photo of the strap.

Saber as carried by an officer on the left side. An enlisted man carried the saber on the right side.

Saber and hanger. The strap and buckle on top of the hanger attaches to a D ring on the saddle. The strap in the middle secures the saber in place, and the strap and buckle to the right goes around the girth.

Above, left: A bayonet frog with a strap to hold the bayonet for mounted personnel. Above, right: A standard bayonet frog.

Two officers on parade in a German town. Both are using the breast strap.

Breast strap dated 1941. This was used to keep the saddle from sliding forward. The breast strap was not used much after February 1940 in an effort to simplify horse equipment.

Ferrier's pouch for draft horses, measuring 12" long by 10.5" wide. The translation of the inside flap label follows:
Contents
Description of Equipment for Shoeing a unmounted (cavalry) horse
1 Handhammer with 300 mm long Handle
1 Hoof mounting Hammer with 325 mm long Handle
50 Hoof nails 350 mm lg.
1 Chisel Spike
1 Rivet Cutting Blade
2 Hoof Knife
2 Hoof Knife Holder
1 Screw Tunneling Slipper 32
1 Hoof Pick 95 mm long
1 Fire Tung 300 mm long
1 Horse Shoeing Pliers with Rivet Fitting Device, 300 mm long

It was essential to establish telephone communications rapidly. Wire was laid over long distances, often from reels on the back of the horse. A rider could have worn the reel while riding the horse, but if the wire got snagged, the results could prove disastrous.

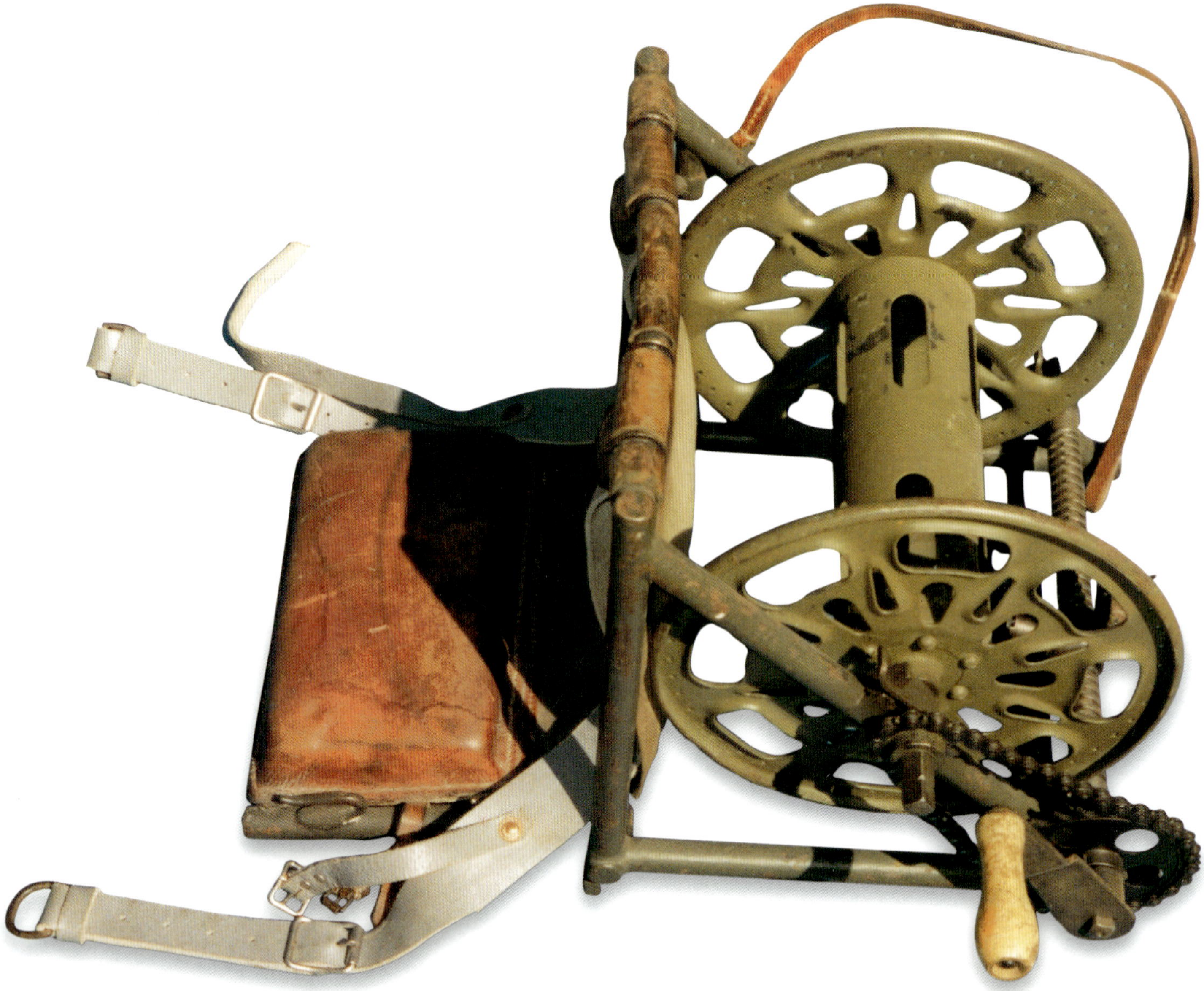

Wire reel.

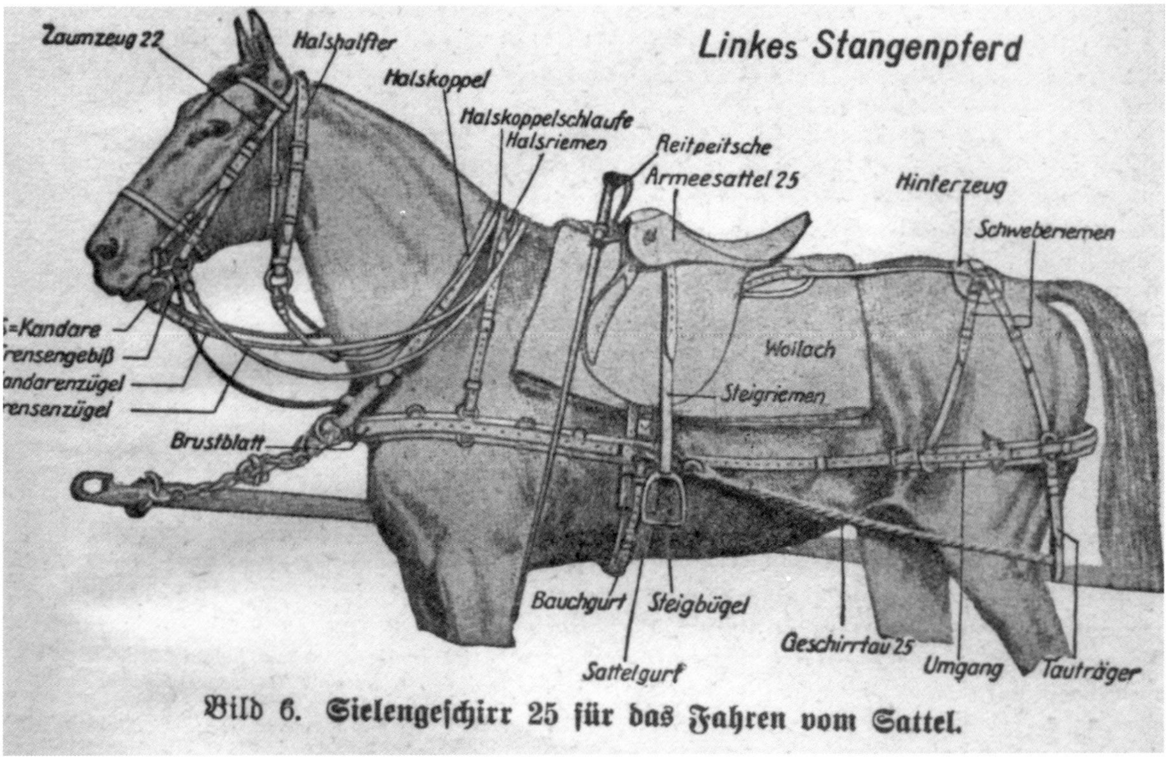

Sielengeschirr 25 breast harness.

Breast harness complete with saddle and M34 saddlebags.

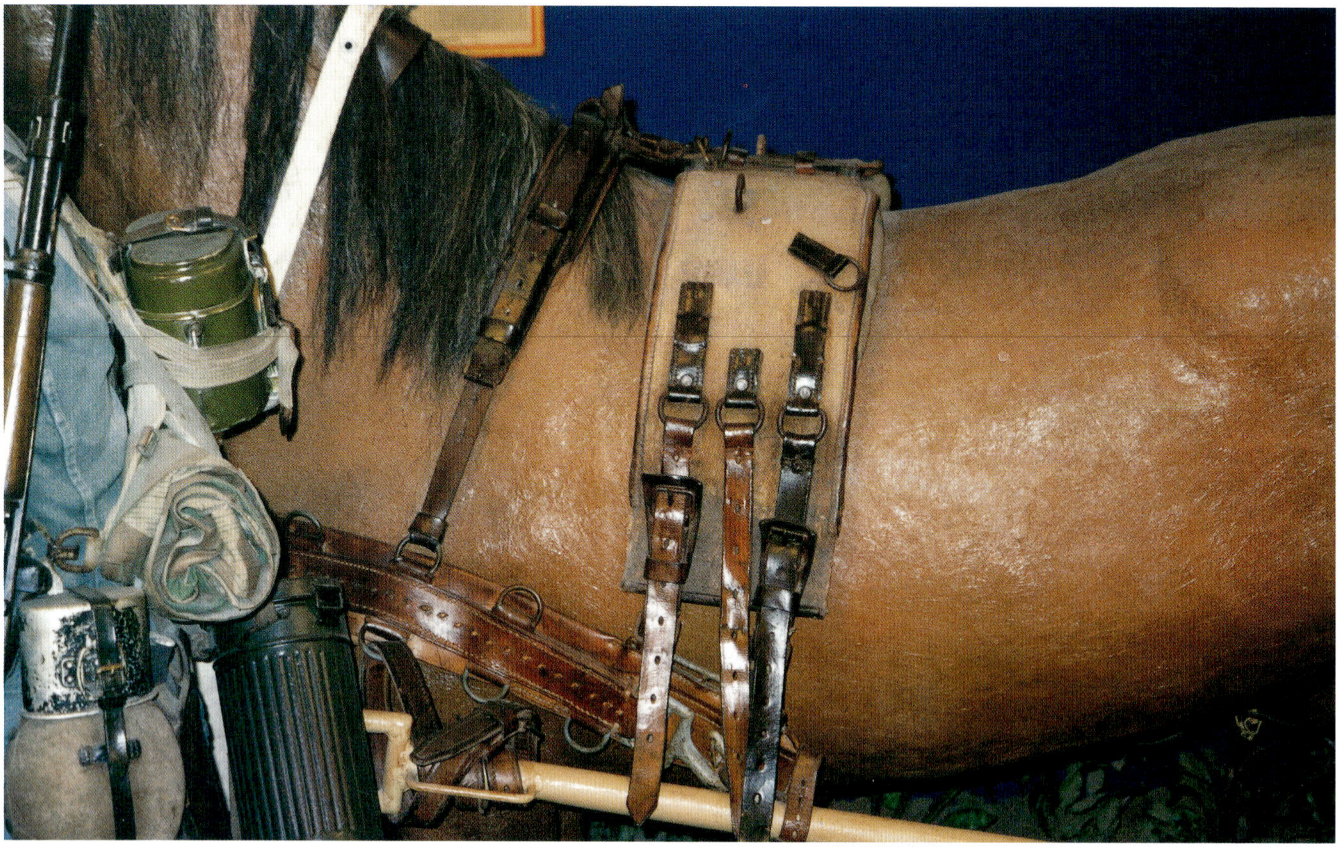

Two photos of a single horse harness taken in a museum in Normandy, France.

Members of an artillery battery stand by a cart drawn by a single horse with a harness similar to the one on the previous page.

Four training manuals. Top left, starting clockwise: The Training of Recruits in Riding, c.1942; Cavalry Primer, c.1935; Horseback Rider Manual, c.1937; The Troop-Horse, c.1938.

Reibert manual, edition for the rider.

An officer in the veterinary service wearing the Horseman's Badge. This badge was introduced in the 1930s by the National Association for Breeding and Testing of German Warm Bloods. It was awarded in three Classes—Bronze, Silver, and Gold—and was based on the completion of riding tests and knowledge of horse care.

Horseman's Badge in gold.

Three photos of Günter Wiswe: first photo is in 1940, when he is an *Unteroffizier*, second two photos he is a cavalry officer in Russia. He is wearing the horseman's badge.

Cardboard tag (6" × 3") showing a horse has been inspected and could be called up for service in the army if needed. This tab was for a heavy draft horse Type II, and it was to be placed on the left side of the halter.

2 | 3

(Eigenhändige Unterschrift des Inhabers — Rufname, Familienname)

I. Angaben zur Person

1	Familienname	Bosse
2	Vornamen (Rufname unterstreichen)	Günther, Heinrich, Albert, Friedrich, Otto
3	Geburtstag, -monat, -jahr	9. April 1913
4	Geburtsort Verwaltungsbezirk (z. B. Kreis, Reg. Bezirk)	Braunschweig
5	Staatsangehörigkeit	reichsdeutsch
6	Religion	ev.
7	Familienstand	led.
8	Beruf (nach Berufsverzeichnis)	erlernter: Landwirt; ausgeübter: Landwirt
9	Eltern	Vater: Wilhelm Bosse (Rufname, Familienname); Bauer (Beruf (nach Berufsverzeichnis)); Mutter: Dina Bosse (Rufname, Familienname); Overbeck (Mädchenname)

This is the *Wehrpass* of a man who joined the cavalry in 1934. He was sent to Russia in May 5, 1942, into an anti-tank company Infantry Regiment 517 (probably due to a lack of remounts). This regiment was part of the 295th Infantry Division. He was killed on September 18, 1942, in Stalingrad.

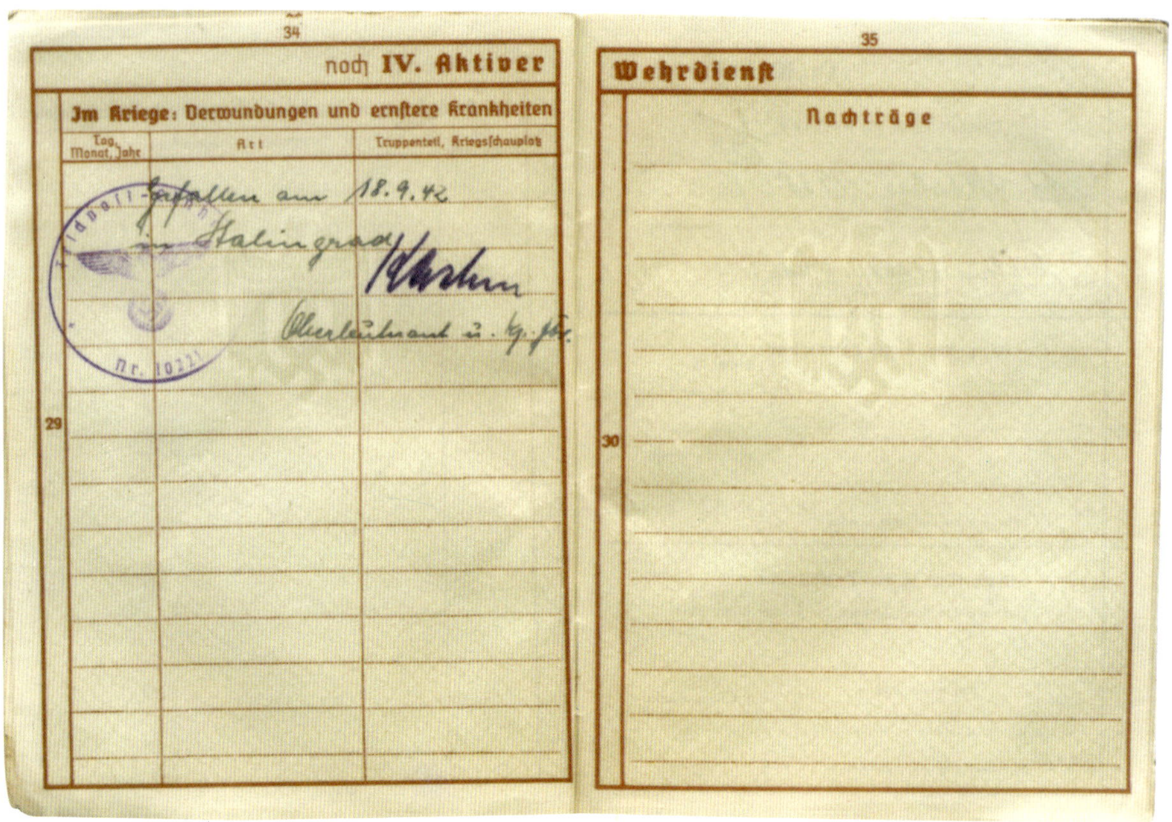

34 | 35

noch **IV. Aktiver** **Wehrdienst**

Im Kriege: Verwundungen und ernstere Krankheiten

Tag, Monat, Jahr	Art	Truppenteil, Kriegsschauplatz
	Gefallen am 18.9.42 in Stalingrad	
	Oberleutnant u. Kp.-Fhr.	

29

Nachträge

30

10

Cavalry in Action

"The Battle Horse." The fourth and most lowly of the knight's horses was given a name that atoned for a multitude of humiliations. It was called the battle horse, which sounds awesome enough. What it really amounted to was a packhorse, an equine trailer. The knight never mounted it. But when he went off to battle, he had to carry extra equipment, weapons to replace broken ones, shields, and some necessary baggage. The battle horse's function was to bear this load, trailing behind with a squire, who sometimes rode it when it was not too heavily laden. In a strict sense, and in spite of its name, the battle horse was merely a workhorse. A self respecting knight would not be seen dead on it." - Arthur Vernon, "The History and Romance of the Horse"

Two Trusting Friends: "In spite of motorization, the cavalry again plays an important role in the war." - Signal Magazine, January 1944

On parade or maneuvers, the infantry officer is at the front of his men. An infantry regiment had 210 horse-drawn wagons, and around 600 horses. Among these were saddle horses for the officers. Later in the war with Russia, these splendid mounts were needed to pull wagons.

An *FH18* 100mm heavy field howitzer being towed though a town in Germany. Because of its weight of 5.5 tons, it was broken down into two parts. The photo at the right is the barrel carriage and the bottom photo is the gun carriage. Even with an eight-horse team this proved too heavy for non-paved roads, much less for the conditions in Russia.

These two photos of horsedrawn as well as motorized equipment marching through a town in Germany. The photo below shows a HF18 barrel trailer being towed by a prime mover.

Pre-war training exercises.

Both photos show a horse-drawn unit on maneuvers in peacetime. The first and second horses in the bottom photo with out riders shows they are carrying M34 saddlebags. At the rear of the saddle is the leather pouch for carrying the mess kit. The pouch was discontinued after February 1940 in an effort to simplify horse equipment.

A sergeant carries an extra pair of boots strapped to his M34 saddlebag. His Kar 98 is in a carbine scabbard carrier that was discontinued at the beginning of the war.

The divisional wagon park getting ready to move out. An Infantry division consisted of 1,743 saddle horses, 3,632 draft horses, and 1,133 horse-drawn vehicles. This number does not count the non-official panje horses and wagons pressed into service. The wagons where divided into two uses. One group was used in direct support of the troops such as carrying weapons, packs, and ammunition. The other group was the supply wagons bringing up the tons of food and supplies from distant railheads or supply depots.

A good example of what a cavalry trooper carried on the back of the saddle. A carbine carrier attached to the troopers belt so when he dismounts he lifts it out of the holder and the rifle is always with him. If he is thrown from his horse in combat he will still have his weapon. Also another reason for this carbine carry device is that it kept the rifle barrel low so it would not catch on branches and pull the rider off his horse. Although it had some advantages, it was somewhat awkward and slow to get the rifle into action. Its use was discontinued in 1941. Also you can see the *zeltbahn* (shelter quarter) strapped on top of the grain forage bag. This bag usually held a blanket to keep it dry and clean but its main purpose was to hold grain for the horse.

A typical HF 1 light field wagon. Because of its lightweight it was very useful in Russia.

Cavalry troops on maneuvers in Germany in 1936. This was part of their on going training.

Two men on a signals equipment limber carrying field telephones and wire reels.

Horse troop line up on side of road on maneuvers in 1936.

Hubertusjagd eines Artillerie-Regiments im Westen

Aufn. PK. Rutkowski-Atlantic (5)

Translation reads. "St. Hubert's Day hunt of at an artillery regiment in the west."

A platoon of leFH 16 (Light Field Howitzers) in the reoccupation of the Rhineland in March 1936.

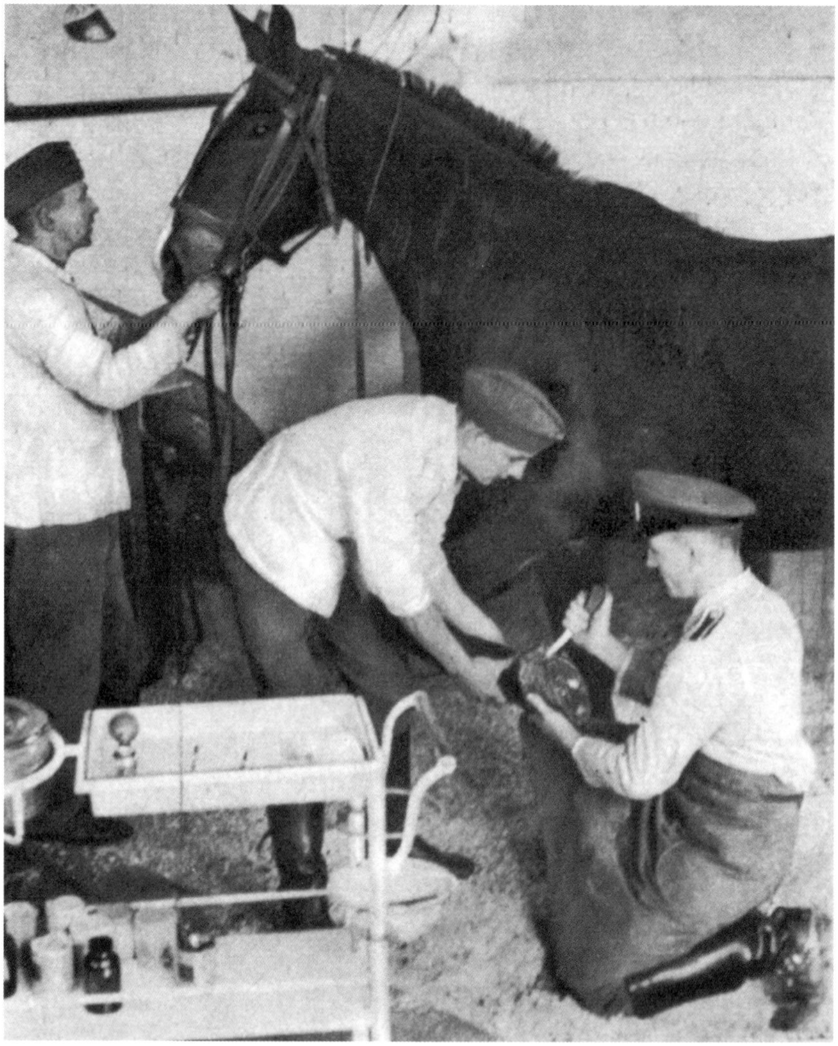

Teaching horseshoeing at an Army school.

This horse has thrown a shoe while on maneuvers. This was not a problem, because every horse carried two pre-fitted shoes: one for the front, and one for the rear hoof. They were carried in the left hand saddlebag, along with eight horseshoe nails.

Interesting photo of the early style girth that was made up of eight hemp cords tan in color held in place by three brown leather reinforcements. It has two buckles on each end to attach the girth to the saddle straps. Also shown is the right M34 saddlebag that could be used as a backpack. Attached to the rear of the saddle is the grain/forage bag. On top of that is the shelter quarter/poncho. On the side of the saddle is the helmet-carrying strap.

A blacksmith in an Infantry Battalion.

A large number of veterinarians and blacksmiths were required to take care of the horses in the German Army. There was never a real problem getting men with these types of skills, because Germany was more familiar with horses than cars in the 1930s and 1940s. Mechanics were much harder to find, and had to be trained.

Caption reads: "At the smithy."

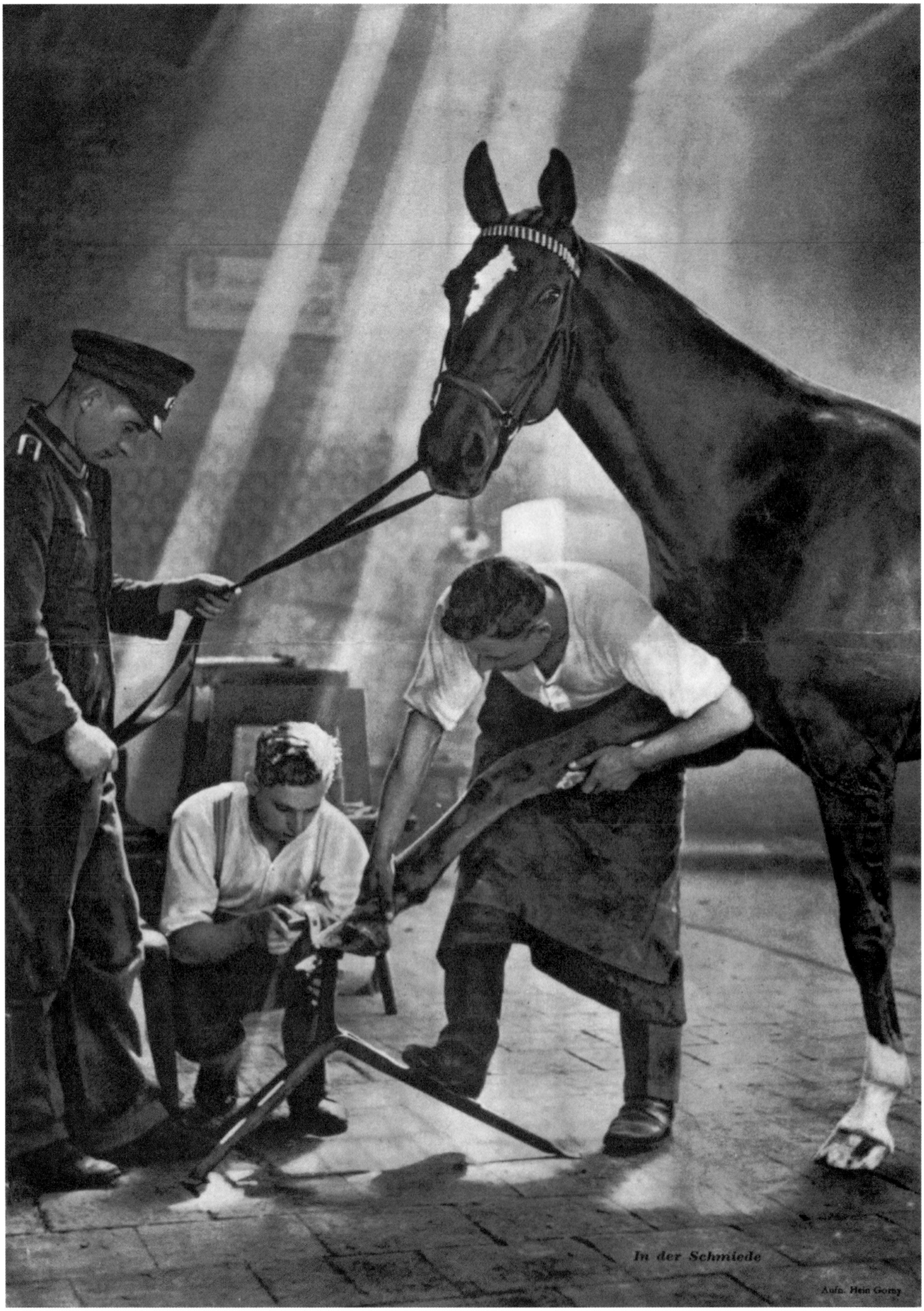

From the back cover of *Deutsche Reiterhefte* magazine. Caption reads: "In der Schmiede" (In the Smithy).

An infantry division, comprised of approximately 1,743 saddle horses and 3,632 draft horses that needed to be shod every six weeks, kept these men very busy.

Parade announcing Freedom of the Nation 1935.

Caption reads: Batteries going into position in difficult terrain.

Reconnaissance troops.

Training a packhorse in the mountains.

A *Hauptfeldwebel* Company 1st Sergeant (*Der Spiess*) admiring a horse. In horse units the *Hauptfeldweble* was called the *Hauptwachtmeister*.

Another Spiess inspecting the soup. While any NCO could hold this position, a NCO with the rank of *Oberfeldwebel* usually held it. His job was similar to that of an American Army Company First Sergeant, but with even more authority. He was often called the "Company Mother," or the *Spiess*, which means Spear, from the time when the senior NCO was armed with a spear. Some but not all of his duties included being in charge of the company headquarters, reports, discipline, promotions, furloughs and, as we can see in the next three pictures, the food. In general he was responsible for the well being of the troops and the overall running of the company. Needless to say, he had an important position and a lot of authority. He could easily be recognized by the two tresses around each cuff. These were referred to as piston rings.

The all-important field kitchen. The soup is being inspected by Der Spiess. In these two pictures the piston rings on his cuffs denoting his position can easily be seen.

The German Army field kitchen nicked named the *Gulaschkonone*, consisted of two parts. The main part contained a large cooking pot and a coffee maker on the side. The second part was the limber that carried food and cooking utensils. This is where the cook and his helper would sit and drive the unit. It was pulled by horses in an Infantry unit and by vehicles in motorized units. At first it was pulled by two horses but the Russian roads proved to difficult for only two horses. The field kitchen could provide food for a company of 120 to 220 soldiers. There was a large and a smaller version of the *Gulaschkonone*. One large advantage of this setup was that soup or stew could be made and kept warm while on the march.

Cleaning the smaller version of the field kitchen. The field kitchens that were horse-drawn had wooden wheels, ones with pneumatic tires were pulled by motor vehicles and some had no wheels and were carried on trucks for faster movement.

Baking oven wagon: This field baking oven provided the 1.5 kilogram "*kommissbrot*" (commissary) bread that was a staple in the soldiers' meal. It also could bake cookies, cakes, and other bakery goods for special occasions.

Dough making wagon.

Both photos show rivers being crossed using pneumatic boats. The top photo the boat is being pulled across and then retrieved by using ropes. In the bottom photo they are going to use the horse as the means of propelling the boat. This is where training paid off. River crossings where conducted at least once a year before the war. But they where always considered dangerous.

Heavy pontoons are brought in position through a forest path by a six-horse team pulling a PF.15 pontoon carrier. The PF.15 weighed 3,747 lbs. empty with a payload of 6,614 lbs., and its overall length was 29 feet six inches.

Horse-drawn supply transport crossing rivers on bridges built by an Engineer Battalion (*Pionier*). These engineers where called "black engineers," referring to the black piping on their shoulder boards.

The soldiers in the bottom photo in the lower right wearing work fatigues are probably *Pioniers* admiring their work.

Crossing a pontoon bridge.

Convoys in the advance on Novgorod.

Maintaining the advance at Pomerania.

At Pomerania during the advance in the Corridor.

To better observe the enemy, the troops dismount and use the embankment for cover.

The task of the mounted reconnaissance: Natural cover, such as forest edges and hollows, is taken advantage of.

After a successful reconnaissance, it goes back at the trot.

Unloading horses at an army field hospital in Poland.

Cavalry troops having mail call in a farmyard in Poland.

The deep sand in Poland made immense demands on men, horses and engines.

Hundreds of horse drawn wagons were the loot from the battles at Andrzejewo.

"For the supplies there are no obstacles."

"A typically Polish street. Soon the German soldiers will create order here."

A supply column crosses a shallow stream in Poland.

Supply convoy crossing a quickly built pontoon bridge in Makow, Poland.

A German cavalry column passes vehicle transport in Poland.

Captions read: "Vehicles and mobile units in the unstoppable advance."

The deep sand and rough terrain in Poland put big requests to horses and man.

Unloading the company wagon and setting up camp. Notice the wire reels, the wire-stringing pole on the ground at far left, and a man on right holding a wire reel. The fur pack on the ground is a telephone installer's pack the two straps on the side held both halves of the wire-stringing pole. Setting up communications was one of the first tasks to be accomplished.

Man unloading personal equipment from company wagon. Notice the mix of fur packs (Tornisters) and canvas rucksacks.

Caption reads: Horse-drawn and motorized convoys secure the supplies. The bad roads in Poland have proven the indispensability of the horse anew.

On the way to the front.

A German supply column stops to inspect a destroyed horse-drawn artillery unit.

Polish cavalry surrendering their horses. After turning in their weapons they are taking their mounts to a collection point. The horses will then be decontaminated and sent on to a hospital section for further evaluation. Healthy horses will be sent to the division's supply section to replace losses in the division. The division supply section had about 130 horses in reserve. Any excess numbers were sent on to the army remount depot for distribution to the Army Group.

Polish prisoners of war turn over Polish cavalry horses to the Germans in the city of Lodz.

Captions read: "Victory parade for the *Führer* in Warsaw."

Above: "With our troops in the West."

"A small incident at the Albert Canal. However the horse is quickly brought to his legs again."

"Cavalry crosses a river in France."

"Destroyed bridges form no obstacle."

"Belgian cavalry marches back after capitulation under the white flag."

"Troop convoys of all formations on the roads of victory."

Caption reads: "German cavalry in the heart of France."

Crossing damaged bridges is always a challenge.

Water must be crossed, bridges or no bridges.

The *Meldereiter* – The Messenger Rider.

Messenger rider at the gallop.

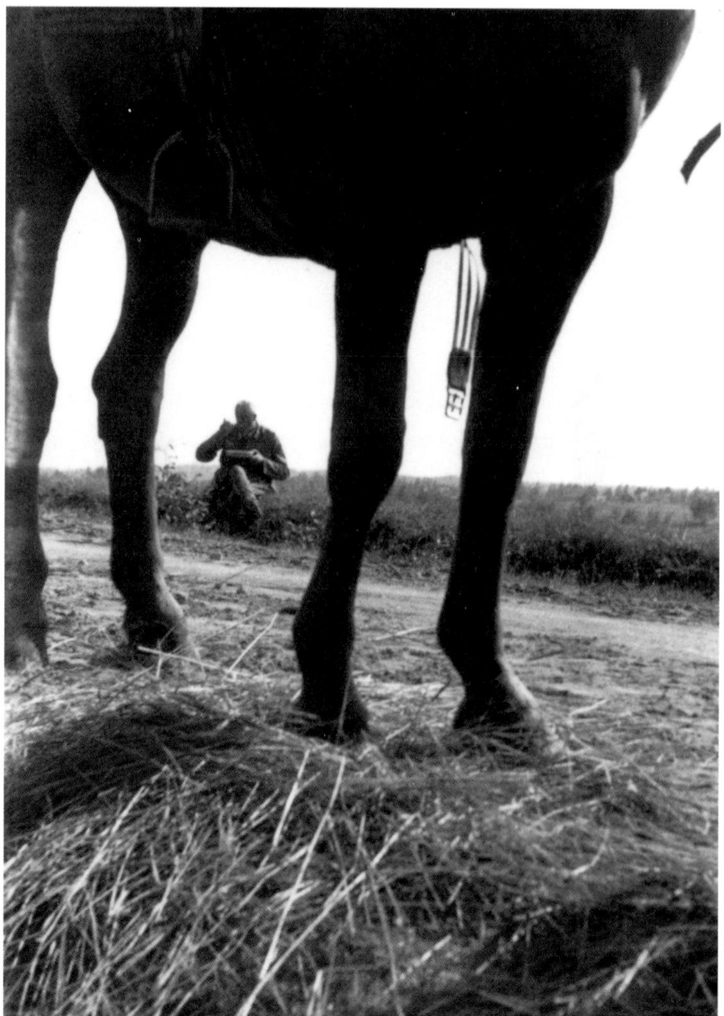

A pause in the march for man and horse.

May 27, 1940, mounted troops moving up towards Dunkirk looking at French prisoners taken just outside of Dunkirk.

The road to Dunkirk is cleared of debris to allow vehicles to continue the advance.

On the road to Paris.

A shrapnel hit before Soissons, France, 7 June 1940.

French prisoners under guard moving back to a collection point past an advancing horse-drawn combat train. June 10, 1940.

French prisoners straggle to the rear past a German column. It is almost certain that the horse pulling the cart with the two French prisoners will be in the service of a new Army, and most likely find itself on the Russian front. It is also almost certain that this horse never returned home to sunny France.

Despondent French troops surrendering to German troops in the town of Verdun, June 15, 1940.

Loading horses onto trains for faster deployment.

France, June 25, 1940: Senior NCOs wait for the unloading of their mounts from a French boxcar.

The next sequence of six photos show horses being loaded into boxcars, usually eight horses to a boxcar. Since horses natural instincts are to flee at the first sign of danger they are inherently afraid of dark and enclosed spaces where they can't flee. Most horses with the trust of their handlers and some training will load easily as in photo #1, and if not, with a little coaxing as in photo #2.

These two photos show a horse that does not want to go into the boxcar. He needs a lot of coaxing, muscle power and a rope around his hindquarters. The rope drives the horse forward and makes the horse feel they have nowhere to go but forward.

These photos show a horse that definitely does not want to load into the boxcar. The combination of the rope, coaxing from the front and rear and a blanket over the horses eyes so he can't see what he is afraid of does the trick.

A French horse-drawn artillery unit is using the front of the town hall of Nancy as a collection point for surrendering, June 16, 1940.

The campaign is over! German troops stop along side of a road to watch French prisoners move to the rear.

Ceasefire! 25 June 1940.

The regimental band leads a victory parade in the field past recently surrendered French troops. The smiling German soldier on the far left in the photo is in sharp contrast to the forlorn looks of the onlooking French.

The war against France is over, time to get caught up on much needed sleep.

An infantry unit on parade through a French town square. As you can see by the dome on the building in the background, these two photos where taken within minutes of each other. From the numbers of onlookers, the parade was not too popular.

Taking a break for a little fun—for the men, at least. A captured donkey at a factory in France is now working for a new master.

It appears by its harness and condition that a German army horse has been harnessed to a locally acquired carriage for a joy ride. The man on the right of the photo is wearing the Brunswick Death's Head of the 13th Cavalry Regiment.

Russia

Infantry and cavalry whistling while on the march, shows the sprit and moral of the troops in the beginning.

Above: A company of infantry comes to a cross road, their mounted officers ask directions from a PK (propaganda kompanie) unit. The photographic truck belongs to the PK unit.

Mounted officer at the head of a long line of infantry looks behind him. He probably turns around because of the sound of a fast approaching motorcycle and sidecar; it may be a dispatch rider with new orders for him.

An officer rides up at a firing range to inspect the progress.

An infantry officer mounted on his personal mount observing his troops as they march along a road that seems to go on endlessly. This is no doubt early in the war. To have a personal mount became a rarity later in the war. The officer is very lucky to have a mount to carry him and his equipment. Later, when a man lost his horse through enemy fire, the elements, or it was needed for other work, the man must have felt his chances of surviving had diminished.

A motorcycle dispatch rider passes a column of marching horseman on a very hot and dusty road.

Men and horses take a well-deserved rest. In the first months of the war, the men and horses tried to keep up with the rapid advance of the armored units. It was a vain attempt to strengthen the ground gained by the tanks and surround the bypassed Russian troops. In many cases, it was impossible to accomplish without motorized infantry.

Cavalry troops moving though forests and cities.

A battery of horse-drawn field howitzers in central Russia advances in the oppressive heat in the summer of 1941.

A mixed column of horse transport and bicycle troops strive to keep up with the rapid advance of the armored units in the summer of 1941.

Having a smoke break while on the march.

Two light supply wagons pose for photos. It seems that they have somehow picked up a cow along the way.

The sign translates, "Keep twenty meters interval between vehicles. Bridge has 10 ton limit."

Raft platforms built on pontoon floats greatly hastened river crossings.

This photo shows a small panje wagon carrying equipment. The back of the photo is captioned, "Russia, 10.7.41." It would seem that the Germans used local horse drawn equipment early on.

I am sure this is a familiar view of Russia to many German soldiers.

When the Germans swept into Russia in June of 1941 with their endless columns of tanks, trucks, and prime movers, they paid scant attention to the Russian peasants, with their small farm carts that were being pulled by the small and scrawny panje horses. As they roared passed them and forcing them off the road they must of though "how primitive". Next to the large German draft horses (as in the photo above) and the sleek and well cared for saddle horses, the panje horses looked somewhat pathetic. When the muddy season came a few months later and even more so when winter stuck this attitude changed. These horses along with their wagons were suddenly in big demand. Motor vehicles failed in the mud and snow of Russia. Only the panje horse could bring up supplies such as food and ammunition to the troops and bring out the wounded. In the thick forests the tracks where to narrow for German wagons but not for the small panje carts. In the middle of winter the only mode of transportation was the panje sleigh. During the first months of 1942 some panzer divisions had as many as 2,000 panje horses, but hardly a single serviceable motor vehicle. The troops gave these panzer divisions the nickname "Panje divisions."

Above and following: These three sequences of photos not only show the road conditions and the use of panje horses and wagons, but also the problems they encountered. Photo one is a HF1 army wagon near the head of the column. Photo two shows a problem developing and photo three further back, the column is a real mess.

Two frontline soldiers inspect a newly captured horse and Cossack saber (shashka) in June 1942. By the way he is holding the saber it can't be too sharp.

Above and following: This dramatic sequence of 24 photos shows a strafing attack from a Sturmovik fighter-bomber. The first photo shows the Russian barn, full of army mounts, before the attack. The next photo shows the thatched roof catching fire. The following photos show the frantic efforts of soldiers trying to lead horses to safety as the barn burns. In a later photo, the soldiers shoot the horses that could not be rescued or were badly burned.

The next sequence of eight photos shows an all too familiar scene in Russia.

In the top photo you have a guy with a stick urging the horses to pull the truck out of a muddy stretch of road. In the bottom photo you can see that the driver of the motorcycle has a stick and is driving the horses. It seems that he plans to use horsepower for some distance.

Both photos show a supply column moving though a Russian village. There were never enough trucks to supply the troops. Most of the trucks were civilian and not designed for the severe weather or horrible road conditions. These horsedrawn supply columns not only had to contend with bad roads, mud and snow, but also partisans or by-passed enemy units. Often these supply columns did not even know where their units were, as they had moved to another sector of the front while on their way to or from the supply depot.

Russian POWs pulling a Kfz.42 signal repair truck up a muddy incline. The team could use four heavy draft horses for this job. Just to the left center of the photo are four German soldiers observing the work. Pushing the company supply wagons loaded with packs and ammunition up a hill. As you can see in the photo the wagons where piled high with equipment.

Pushing the company supply wagons loaded with packs and ammunition up a hill. As you can see in the photo the wagons where piled high with equipment.

3oth photos show vehicles being pushed or pulled down the main street of a Russian village. One by manpower, the other by horsepower. The top photo ıas German soldiers, Russians, and even a German officer pushing.

A Mercedes-Benz 320 being pulled by two horses. Another two horses can be seen to the left of the road if additional horsepower is needed.

The German automobile industry could not manufacture enough trucks to make the army fully motorized. To relieve this shortage, they used captured French and Czech trucks. Most of the German, French, Czech, and other captured vehicles were of civilian design and unsuitable for the rigors of the Russian campaign. The Germans went into Russia with over 2,000 different types of vehicles – making maintenance a logistical nightmare. According to German Army calculations, Russia was invaded with a shortage of over 2,700 trucks. As the campaign wore on, mechanical transportation shortages due to wear and tear increased. These shortages were solved in part by the use of horses.

Civilian cars where not up to the rigors of Russian roads. In the background is a prime mover coming to the rescue.

Above: Repairing a front axle in the field. Below: Replacing the front shoes of a horse in the field. These are very different tasks but I can see some commonality. Horrible road conditions and vast travel distances in Russia made field maintenance a real challenge. Bringing up supplies was so vital and constant that it put a huge strain on motor vehicles, horses, and men. Imagine doing these maintenance jobs in winter!

The spring thaw soon made the primitive roads impassable. The constant traffic of trucks and wagons churned the mud into a quagmire. In the bottom photo, a light field howitzer goes off the road to avoid the muddy conditions, and still gets stuck.

Only the corduroy roads made many operations in the swampy forests, mud of spring and autumn in central and northern Russia possible. Hundreds of miles of corduroy road had to be built during the muddy seasons in order to move up supplies and heavy equipment. The crossing of the many small swamps found along almost any Russian road caused serious delays. At these points logs about ten inches in diameter had to be cut and placed sometimes in many layers. While these improvised roads made travel possible it also made these spots bottle necks. These roads were just wide enough for one truck because longer logs could not be procured. Since they were the only arteries for troop movements and supply traffic they were used day and night and their maintenance presented many problems. The vehicles as well as the foot soldiers had to slow down. Traveling along a corduroy road on foot or by motor was very strenuous, and the constant bouncing was hard on equipment. Note the civilian license plate on this truck.

Saar-58860
WH

A variety of horsedrawn wagons pressed into service to get the supplies through.

Supply column next to a column of Russian prisoners.

The following sequence of four photos shows a lFK 16 light field piece on maneuvers. Its rate of fire was eight to ten rounds per minute.

Even this relatively light field piece had to be manhandled at times.

A ford is crossed.

Bringing up the rear.

An HF1, which stood for Army light field wagon with a four-horse team proved to be the most versatile in bad terrain.

Two HF1s ford a stream. An empty HF1 weighed approximately 1,350 lbs. and could carry approximately 1,650 lbs of payload.

A HF1 light field wagon being pulled by a four-horse team. A man on horseback took the photo; you can see his shadow in the lower right hand corner.

The same type wagon pulled by a two-horse team is about to be stuck. Even the light field wagon pulled by two horses was not sufficient horsepower for Russian roads.

Both of these photos are dated September 5, 1941. They probably were taken to show the folks back home how primitive the farm carts were. This was less than three months into the war with Russia; little did this photographer know how importation this type of transportation would become.

Part of a Bicycle Reconnaissance Unit riding alongside their mounted counter part.

A wagonload of bicycles is being brought to a railhead to be returned to Germany. The bad roads in Russia made the bicycles useless in winter and the spring and autumn mud.

Mounted reconnaissance on a mission in Russia, dated June 1941.

A column stops along a river's edge to adjust saddles and equipment.

These two pictures show a mounted column taking a noonday break to rest and feed the horses. Although the men in the foreground are taking a break, the men in the background are taking care of the horses, which needed constant attention.

Caption reads: "Cossack Voluntary Police on a patrol."

"Soldiers and locals find the Cossacks wearing the traditional uniforms interesting. Cossacks still wear the old fur caps and famous uniforms, which not only do our soldiers find interesting, but also the local inhabitants." - *Die Wehrmacht* magazine, September 1942.

Cossack militia. They take care of order in the area and act as guides for our soldiers into the forests and mountain-ways of the Caucasus.

Riding past the graves of their fallen comrades, a party of released Greek soldiers make their way back to their homes.

Bulgarian reservists on their way to report in.

Constant activity at the Danube river ferries.

Two soldiers have pressed into service a small donkey to carry their gear.

Makeshift sled pulled by a panje horse serves as a soup wagon. The soup server in the middle has towels tucked in his belt to keep from spilling soup on his coat. Soldier on the right wears the Iron Cross 2nd Class ribbon. By the way they are dressed, it is cold, but they have no idea of what lies ahead.

A HF1 slipped off the icy road and tipped over. In this first winter of the war, the troops are only dressed in overcoats and are wearing the M34 field cap with the sides pulled over their ears. This is not a very warm combination, especially for a Russian winter. The shortest man in the photo is a HIWI, a captured Russian who has volunteered to help the Germans. He is wearing a Russian winter fur hat (ushanka) with the ear flaps pulled down—a much more suitable hat for Russian winters.

Again, poorly dressed soldiers with Russian horses and wagons during the beginning of the first Russian winter.

Bringing supplies on a sled to a village were the troops at least had shelter.

Local farm, or in some cases makeshift sleds, provided major transportation.

An officer and a four-man crew with their light field howitzer mounted on a makeshift sled.

During Operation Barbarossa (the invasion of Russia) the German Army lost 75,000 motor vehicles and these losses could not be made up by the German motor vehicle industry. Horses had to fill in the gaps when and wherever possible.

Russia, spring 1942. A long column of troops climb a steep grade with pack horses bring up the rear. Notice the bicycle in right hand corner.

Narrow bridges are crossed without any hesitancy from the horses.

Horses are loaded onto trains.

A short meal rest is taken during the advance.

An SS column on the march. Notice the horses are wearing ear-protecting hats in the picture below.

SS horsemen in the vastness of Russia.

SS troops being inspected. Notice the protective cover on the left leg of the man on the far right. This was used to protect the foot of wagon drivers from the wagon's beam.

Checking the bridle while a mounted friend holds the reins just out of the photo.

Elements of the SS Cavalry Regiment 1 crossing the Pripet River on 8 September 1941 during operations against partisans.

Early in the war, long columns of camouflaged wagons and infantry advancing through a town in central Russia.

This photo shows a mixture of transportation including civilian cars pressed into service. These vehicles would not hold up for very long under the climate and road conditions of Russia.

An endless line of mixed transport consisting of trucks, bicycles, horsedrawn equipment and mounted horsemen advance in central Russia, 1941.

A cavalry horse troop in the summer of 1941 in central Russia.

A horse troop consisting of approximately 180 men on the steppes of Russia.

Advancing into the seemingly endless steppes.

The endless steppe of Russia.

For many, it proved too much.

Russians bury dead horses under guard.

Result of a road shelling. If one horse in a harnessed team was killed, it immobilized the entire team.

The results of a shelling. Apparently the horse is not the only casualty; a medic has been called for.

This photo is from the same grouping as the one above. A group has gathered to watch the preparation of tonight's supper.

Back of photograph says, "Visiting the grave of my horse. I hope my new mount is as good."

Infantry support wagons, including a field kitchen (first wagon on the left) taking a break for washing and maintenance.

After a brief rest they are harnessing the teams for the continued road march.

Six horse teams were used to pull the heavier weapons as well as some of the heavy combat vehicles. The type 25 breast harness being used on a two-horse team for a HF1 light field wagon.

The type 25 breast harness being used on a two-horse team for a HF1 light field wagon.

A light field howitzer 18 and crew being towed by a six-horse team.The leFH 18 was the standard field howitzer in the German army till the end of the war. It was 105 caliber weighed 4,377 lbs. and was approximately 11 feet long. It had a range of 11,674 yards. In 1936 the wooden wheels and spokes were replaced with light metal wheels with 12 spoke hand holes as pictured above to help manhandle the gun into position.

These two photos show two of the conditions that had to be endured, rain and heat. The top photo also shows the spare wheel to the right of the photo. This spare wheel was carried on the rear of the HF1 and HF2 ammunition and supply wagons.

A Light field howitzer 16. Although the leFH16 was used as early as WWI it was the standard divisional howitzer until the leFH18 was introduced in 1935. The leHF16 was used in all theaters until the end of the war.

Troops enter Kharkov at the end of October 1941. The soldier at the far left of the photo sitting on a chair holding his head in his hands seems to typify how exhausted the troops have become.

Above: Leading horses out of the city to grass land for grazing and rest.

On the advance through a Latvian landscape.

Attention, mines on the street!

Caption reads: "Supply convoy in the east."

Caption reads: "Supplies for the Grenadier Companies."

Caption reads: "Infantry Signals wagon in the advance."

Caption reads: "Covered artillery on the advance."

Caption reads: "Mounted reconnaissance troops on patrol."

Caption reads: "Grenadier company supply train on the advance."

Mounted Infantry.

Ammunition convoys of the infantry follow the troops right into the front lines.

After forming a skirmish line, the horses are brought back to cover by the horse holders.

A Cavalry reconnaissance troop at the point.

Caption reads: "On the heels of the fleeing enemy."

The supply and combat train of an infantry division prior to 1944 consisted of 1,133 wagons, 3,632 draft horses and 1,743 saddle horses. This column seems to stretch on endlessly as it advances into central Russia in 1941.

Taking a break for the men and horses after reaching the top of a long and steep grade.

Heavy draft horses being loaded onto trucks to save time, improve speed, and conserve the horses. Wounded horses were evacuated to horse hospitals. Replacement horses were in such demand; they were driven to their units either from remount collection points or from horse hospitals as soon as they recovered.

Captions read: Machine gun section.

On the march, it was recommended a cavalryman ride for fifty minutes, then dismount and walk for ten minutes to give the horse a rest (conditions permitting).

Panje wagons in the service of the Army.

July 1941 with Army Group South on the endless steppes of Russia. The dust kicked up by the advancing column caked the men until they looked like white statues. Not only did the men develop respiratory problems from the dust, but also the horses. The coughing of men and horses replaced the sound of troops singing marching songs.

Cavalry NCO riding seemingly alone in the vast steppes of Russia. Notice the helmet hung from the saddle by the helmet-carrying strap.

Caption reads: "Horses and vehicles advancing, always advancing. July 1941."

Caption reads: "Riders, bicycle troops, vehicles and mobile units in the unstoppable advance. July 1941."

Horses are used to bring warm meals to the fighting troops. Here a solder is loading a horse with a (*Essenbehalter*) hot food container. Usually they contained soup or stew.

Caption reads: "While the supply convoys pass by in the heat on the dusty road, the motorcycle dispatch rider returns in order to convey important news of the sector."

Horsedrawn artillery on the advance as they pass Soviet prisoners.

A telephone construction wagon goes forward at the gallop.

Unending convoys closely follow the fighting troops.

Caption reads: In some places the deep sand seems like it has no end.

Caption reads: "Major General Lancelle salutes his brave Infantry Division." The motto of the Division is "There where the General is, is the front."

Captions read: "The guns of the heavy artillery are brought up through deep sand into the ordered positions."

Artillery moves forward through deep sand without hesitating.

Above: Enveloped in dense dust from the battle the troops follow.

Right: Field Kitchen and unending supply convoys march east in the glowing, sunbathing heat.

Caption reads: "Heavy artillery on the advance in the east."

Caption reads: "At the Village Well."

"With each rest, the first concern is for the horses." – cavalry standard procedure.

An officer at a well in the Ukraine 1941. Horses required a lot of water. The amount would depend on it's size, environmental temperature, and amount of moisture in the feed and, of course, how hard they are working. In general a horse would require six to ten gallons of water a day. A large draft horse pulling a wagon or artillery piece on the steppes of Russia in July would require a lot more. In northern and central Russia, the villages had ample wells with fresh water. In southern Russia water supply was much scarcer.

A typical Russian village well.

Both photos show men and horses at a village draw well that was typical throughout Russia. A lot of time was spent at these wells quenching the thirst of the men and horses. The water had to be drawn up in a bucket that was very time consuming. Due to the lack of accurate maps, the distance to the next village was unknown.

Getting water for both man and beast was always a priority.

Caption reads: "Hungarian Cavalry in the East." This officer at the head of the column does not seem to be happy with the situation. His mood probably didn't change for the better, since this photo was taken in October 1941.

Hungarian cavalry unit. September 1941.

Supply column of Italian mountain troops. September 1941.

Caption reads: A hillside is taken at the trot.

The darling of the squadron. Notice the emblem of the 1st Cavalry Division later the 24th Panzer Division on the side of the limber.

The field kitchen follows the Regiment.

Caption reads: "Horse and Motor: One is as important as the other. There are even cases, in which the horse achieves services that cannot be achieved by the motor in a modern war."

Six-horse artillery team pulls a Horch out of the mud. Notice the dead horse next to the vehicle.

Peeling potatoes.

Pulling an HF7 all steel company wagon up a hill in sandy conditions. This wagon was much too heavy for the conditions in Russia. There are other photos of this wagon being pulled and pushed by the men of the company. Its excessive weight not only took its toll on the horses, but also on the men.

A signals platoon with a six-horse team on the steppes of Russia.

Six horse team passing a disabled T34/76 tank in Russia 1941.

These two pictures show the HF 7 all-steel wagon. The top photo shows it on a paved European road were it could be easily pulled by two horses. But in the rough road conditions of Russia, the all-steel construction proved far too heavy. This wagon was nicknamed "the horse killer."

Mud in the fall and spring and dust in summer, all had to be overcome by horse and manpower.

Both photos show an ammunition column moving though a burning city in Russia.

The trooper with the white horse has the older model strand girth, it was made up of eight strands held together by three leather keepers. They were supposed to be eventually replaced by the web girth.

Caption reads: "Without highway or bridge, they go across country, according to the yielding enemy."

Passing a knocked out Russian BT series light tank with Army Group Center July 1941.The infantry unit in the center background trying to keep up with the advance of the armored units (which was impossible).

Mounted reconnaissance unit passes a destroyed BT-5 light Russian tank on the outskirts of Kiev. Notice the flag in the center of the photo; it would be interesting to see what flag it is.

German cavalry passing an abandon Russian BT-7 tank. The BT-7 had 20mm frontal armor and a 45mm gun. By the time this early war photo was taken the BT-7 was antiquated.

A fox hole for horses.

With some success, Finnish troops put into service a summer sled to haul food containers.

Bringing up supplies was always a problem. Here German troops bring up supplies through a forest in panje wagons. Hiwis are helping or maybe acting as guides.

Mixed transport including trucks, horses, and bicycles stop for a rest in southern Russia 1942.

Cavalry troops ride through bombed and burning cities while trying to keep pace with the armored units.

Every mode of transportation was used in Russia. This photo shows a car partly obscured by two horses, a mounted soldier to the left of photo, a horse drawn-wagon and thrown on top of the wagon a bicycle.

Three NCOs following a supply wagon that looks like it's hauling hay. That maybe why the horses are following so closely. The one soldier is equipped with binoculars, bayonet, canteen, and is using his bread bag as another saddlebag.

Supply wagons with escorts: Bring supplies from railheads or supply depots up to their units was usually a long and dangerous job, also their units might of changed positions while they were gone and not easily found given the bad roads and poor maps. Sometimes these convoys were ambushed and wiped out. One supply wagon driver compared the experience of riding through the forests in small convoys, as like the American Wild West movies, we were the settlers and the partisans the Indians.

A railroad track repair crew. A Hiwi leading a horse that is pulling a railroad cart containing their tools. This picture shows how horses where utilized when ever possible. Burying detail going about their grim work. Even the horse seems affected with sorrow.

Horses put to another use.

A typical Russian farm cart pulled by one panje horse down the main street of a Russian village. Not exactly heroic, but it beats walking in the mud.

Above and following: Tracked vehicles have not as yet passed down this road creating deep ruts and making it even harder to get through. This sequence of five photos shows the typical challenge of driving a wagon during the muddy season.

Clear of the mud and on firmer ground, for the time being.

These two photos show the Russian type harness. When the Germans used panje wagons and horses, the harness equipment was unusually in poor condition and in need of repair. The poor horse in the bottom photo looks in need of repair also.

Giving the horse a break.

Non-standard army transportation. (but it's better than walking.)

Artillery-team horses being led out of the immediate area after their gun has been set up in a defensive position.

A horse-drawn column stops to observe action up ahead.

Short rest and a campfire. A horse-drawn artillery team starts to eat their supper around a campfire. Only after they have picketed, fed and watered the horses, can they see to their own comforts.

This photo shows Gebirgsj%oger (mountain troops) in the Caucasus with Army Group South in the summer of 1942. In the foreground is a MG34 with a drum that held a fifty round belt of ammunition (Gurttrommel 34) laying on top of the wagon. A full strength mountain division consisted of 13,056 men. It also had 447 motorcycles and 858 motor vehicles of all sizes. But because its main mission was fighting in mountains and rugged terrain, it had 714 horsedrawn carts and 3,506 horses and mules.

Crossing a fast-moving mountain stream.

Both photos show *Gebirgsjägers* bringing supplies and equipment up the most difficult terrain.

Three photos taken in the cold mountain mist show Gebirgsj‰gers bring up a 75mm mountain howitzer and ammunition. This gun was used widely by mountain troops. Although the gun weighed 1,351 lbs., it could be broken down into seven animal loads. It had a range of 7,270 yards. And each shell weighed twelve pounds. It could fire high explosive, hollow charge, shrapnel, and armor piercing rounds.

A horse-drawn unit that stretches far into the distance passes Russian peasants who are fleeing their village.

Only women, children and old men are left. All able-bodied men have been conscripted into the Russian Army.

Russian refuges take to the road carrying their few possessions. The child at the left of the photo is carrying a samovar probably the family's most prized possession.

Caption reads: The battle of Stalingrad has fully erupted. From north, west and south the German divisions in heavy fighting have fought their way into the fortress-belt and have repressed the Soviets into a narrow area. Continually air force and artillery hammer on the city that is wrapped in a dense smoke-cloud. Stalingrad, the heart of the Soviet Union has become a burning hell. In unending convoys of supplies and new troops roll over quickly erected pontoon bridges in the direction of Stalingrad.

The disastrous retreat from the Don. Using any transportation that could be found, German troops head west.

Going up a small incline on an icy and rutted road proves to be difficult. At the bottom of the road, a vehicle seems to be stuck.

Even with winter clothes, blankets and a sled insulated with a bed of hay, these soldiers look miserable.

A convoy of sleighs pulled by oxen and driven by Hiwis (Russian auxiliary volunteers) they are wearing armbands on their Russian overcoats to show that they are in the service of the German Army. Many Russian volunteers from prisoner-of-war camps were employed as auxiliaries to replace soldiers transferred into front line units from supply and service units. In general they were quite dependable and useful.

During sever snowstorms sleds were frequently the only means of transportation.

These troops appear miserable as they move supplies to the front with temperatures at -45° Fahrenheit.

Reconnaissance squadron at a river crossing.

Horse and bicycle mounted troops on the march.

Cavalry troops admiring a Ju 88 bomber.

Off loading Ju 52s at a supply depot in Russia onto horse-drawn transport in April 1943.

The ubiquitous HF7 company wagon. It is not only carrying the company packs and equipment but also hay for bedding until the horses ate it all, which would not take long.

Late in the war, horses became harder to come by. As can be seen in this photo the company wagon normally pulled by a team of two horses has only one horse to do the job.

A horse looks at his teammate who died in harness while four dejected soldiers look on.

At a re-enactment the author looks at other less reliable modes of transportation.

Military experts agree that horses no longer have a place in modern warfare. Department of Defense U.S. Special Forces troops ride horseback as they work with members of the Northern Alliance in Afghanistan during Operation Enduring Freedom on November 12, 2001. Maybe we shouldn't turn in our spurs just yet. DoD photo

Bibliography

Angolia, John R./Shlicht, Adolf. *Uniforms and Traditions of the German Army, 1933-1945.* San Jose, California: R. James Bender Publishing. 1987.

Bayer, Hanns. *Kavallerie – Divisionen der Waffen-SS.* Osnabr¸ck, Germany: Munin-Verlag GmbH, 1982.

Beevor, Antony. *Stalingrad: The Fateful Siege: 1942-1943.* New York, New York: Viking Penguin, 1998.

Buchner, Alex. *The German Infantry Handbook 1939-1945.* West Chester, Pennsylvania: Schiffer Publishing, Ltd., 1991.

Devereaux, Frederick L. *The Cavalry Manual of Horse Management.* Cranbury, New Jersey: A.S. Barnes And Company, Inc., 1979.

Die Wehrmacht. 7 Jahrgang, Nr. 13. Berlin, German, den 16. June 1943.

Die Woche. Berlin, Germany, 15 May 1940.

DiNardo, R. L. *Mechanized Juggernaut or Military Anachronism? Horses and the German Army of World War II.* New York, New York: Greenwood Press, 1991.

Engelmann, Joachim. *German Heavy Field Artillery 1934-1945.* Atglen, Pennsylvania: Schiffer Publishing Ltd., 1995.

Englelmann, Joachim. *German Light Field Artillery 1934-1945.* Atglen, Pennsylvania: Schiffer Publishing Ltd., 1995.

H Div.11/2 *Das Truppenferd.* Berlin, Germany: Berlag, von E.G., Rittler & Gohn, 1938.

H Div. 12 *Reitervorschrift (R.B.).* Berlin, Germany: Berlag, von E.G., Rittler & Gohn, 1937.

Hillebrand-Mueller, Burkhart Generalmajor. *MS # P-090, Horses in the German Army 1941-1945.* U.S. Army Military History Institute, Historical Division, Headquarters, United States Army, Europe, Foreign Military Studies Branch.

Lucas, James. *German Army Handbook.* Sutton Publishing 2002.

Mitcham, Samuel W. Jr. *Hitler's Legions. The German Army Order of Battle, World War II.* Stein and Day 1985.

Piekiewicz, Janusz. *The Cavalry of World War II.* Briarcliff Manor, New York: Stein and Day, 1979.

Remounts, Acclimation and Breeds, U.S. Government Manuscript D-099

Richter, Christian Klaus. *Cavalry of the Wehrmacht 1941-1945.* Atglen, Pennsylvania: Schiffer Publishing Ltd., 1995.

Richter, Christian Klaus. *Die Feldgrauen Reiter.* Augsburg, Germany: Weltbild Verlag, GmbH and Company, 1994.

Schaefer L. & Siefert K., Dr.s, *Horses in the Russian Campaign: Forage, Feeding, Water, and Watering Conditions, as well as Preparations for the Winter.* US Government Manuscript D-097 5 May 1947.

Schaefer L. & Siefert K., Dr.s,: *The Veterinary Service During the Campaign in the East.* US Government Manuscript D-096 April 1947.

Signal Magazine. Nr. 21, 1 Novembre 1941, Deutscher Verlag: Berlin Germany.

Tier und Naturfreund. 2 Jahrgang, Nr. 4, April 1937, Stuttgart, Germany.

United States War Department Technical Manual TM-E 30-451. Handbook on German Military Forces. War Department 15 March 1945.

Von Haugk, Siegfried. *Die Ausbildung der Rekruten im Reiten.* Berlin, Germany: Verlag, von E.G., Rittler & Gohn, 1942.

Notes

1 Armored infantry

2 "Panye" (sometimes rendered "panje") is a German Army adaptation of a Polish word applied to the common, small Russian and Polish farm horses and the vehicles and sleds, which they pulled.

3 *Panzergruppe*: An armored force of army size operating in conjunction with an army.

4 Supervising veterinary officers were the senior veterinary officers on the headquarters staffs of army groups, armies, corps, and divisions.